Leveraging Socio-Emotional Assessment to Foster Children's Human Rights

Leveraging Socio-Emotional Assessment to Foster Children's Human Rights focuses on teaching and assessing students' social and emotional attributes within the broader context of children's rights. School teachers are charged with more than just academic development – every day, they have opportunities to guide children toward humanistic, justice-orientated perspectives and to serve as role models and relationship-builders. Built from a growing body of research on the benefits of socio-emotional learning and assessment in classrooms, this book prepares pre-service and in-service teachers to take on the shifting mindset that is required for learning processes that promote dignity and respectful relations in the classroom. These concise, accessible chapters address the value and effects of positive student-teacher relationships, classroom implementation and assessment methods, student- and parent-inclusive feedback and more.

Jacqueline P. Leighton is Full Professor in the Department of Educational Psychology at the University of Alberta, Canada, and a Registered Psychologist.

Student Assessment for Educators
Edited by James H. McMillan,
Virginia Commonwealth University, USA

Using Formative Assessment to Support Student Learning Objectives
M. Christina Schneider and Robert L. Johnson

Managing Classroom Assessment to Enhance Student Learning
Nicole Barnes and Helenrose Fives

Using Differentiated Classroom Assessment to Enhance Student Learning
Tonya R. Moon, Catherine M. Brighton, and Carol A. Tomlinson

Leveraging Digital Tools to Assess Student Learning
Stephanie Smith Budhai

Using Grading to Support Student Learning
Matt Townsley

Leveraging Socio-Emotional Assessment to Foster Children's Human Rights
Jacqueline P. Leighton

For more information about this series, please visit: https://www.routledge.com/Student-Assessment-for-Educators/book-series/SAFE

Leveraging Socio-Emotional Assessment to Foster Children's Human Rights

Jacqueline P. Leighton

Routledge
Taylor & Francis Group

NEW YORK AND LONDON

Cover image: ©Getty/oxygen

First published 2023
by Routledge
605 Third Avenue, New York, NY 10158

and by Routledge
4 Park Square, Milton Park, Abingdon, Oxon, OX14 4RN

Routledge is an imprint of the Taylor & Francis Group, an informa business

Library of Congress Cataloging-in-Publication Data
Names: Leighton, Jacqueline P., author.
Title: Leveraging socio-emotional assessment to foster children's human
rights / Jacqueline P. Leighton.
Description: New York, NY: Routledge, 2022. |
Series: Student assessment for educators | Includes bibliographical
references and index.
Identifiers: LCCN 2022012200 (print) | LCCN 2022012201 (ebook) |
ISBN 9780367712686 (hardback) | ISBN 9780367715984 (paperback) |
ISBN 9781003152781 (ebook)
Subjects: LCSH: Affective education. | Social learning. | Emotions in children. |
Teacher-student relationships. | Classroom environment. | Children's rights.
Classification: LCC LB1072 .L456 2022 (print) | LCC LB1072 (ebook) |
DDC 370.15/34—dc23/eng/20220427
LC record available at https://lccn.loc.gov/2022012200
LC ebook record available at https://lccn.loc.gov/2022012201

ISBN: 9780367712686 (hbk)
ISBN: 9780367715984 (pbk)
ISBN: 9781003152781 (ebk)

DOI: 10.4324/9781003152781

Typeset in Sabon
by codeMantra

To my mother and father, my beloved teachers, for showing me how to walk in the strength of human rights and freedoms by leaving Chile's Pinochet Dictatorship when I was 4 years old

Contents

Acknowledgments

Preparation of this book was supported by a grant to the author from the Social Sciences and Humanities Research Council of Canada (SSHRC Grant No. 435-2016-0114). Grantees undertaking such projects are encouraged to express freely their professional judgment. This book, therefore, does not necessarily represent the positions or the policies of the Canadian government, and no official endorsement should be inferred. I wish to extend my heartfelt gratitude to Dr. James H. McMillan for the invitation to contribute to the series of Student Assessment for Educators, his careful and thoughtful feedback on all parts of the book, with any errors or omissions being entirely my own. I also want to extend a sincere thank you to Daniel Schwartz, Editor of Education at Routledge, for the gift of extra time in writing this during the challenge of the current times.

1

Assessing for Wellness and Children's Rights

This book has a simple goal: That by the time you finish reading it, you will recognize three relatively simple psychological principles about student learning and assessment. Many of you will know these three principles intuitively given your interactions over many years with the children you know and teach. However, what you may not know about intuitively is the growing level of *empirical research* that supports these three principles. Knowing about the empirical research that supports these principles will allow you to better understand why your practice is useful, how to respond when people question you about your practice and most importantly how to enrich the lives of your students. These principles are aligned within a broader view of children's basic human rights in the learning domains they inhabit.

This chapter begins with some of the basics – working definitions, scope of assessment tools and rationale for considering assessment alongside children's human rights. Although

DOI: 10.4324/9781003152781-1

this book cannot cover or cite the broad research literature on the subject of social and emotional assessment, and children's human rights, the chapter includes some of the most germane, rigorous and lucid works in support of the principles presented.

Before we delve into the details of this work, an important idea must be kept in mind throughout while reading the chapters. The idea is this: *children's social and emotional readiness and wellness does not begin or end in the classroom.* Children's social and emotional health is affected by many environments. Bronfenbrenner's *Bioecological model* (Bronfenbrenner & Ceci, 1994) shown in Figure 1.1 is often used to guide

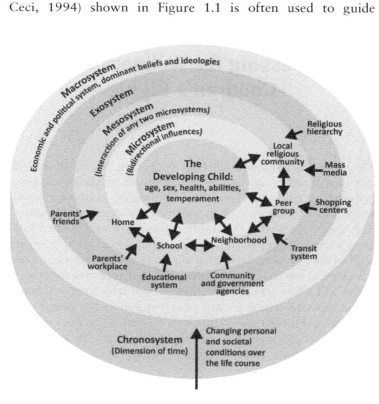

Figure 1.1 Urie Bronfenbrenner's Bioecological Systems Model. Image by Ian Joslin is licensed under CC BY 4.0.

psychological and even medical practitioners in understanding human development generally and in supporting children's physical and mental wellness specifically (Hamwey, Allen, Hay & Varpio, 2019). Figure 1.1 shows that there are many environmental systems that impact the child. The microsystem impacts the child directly (e.g., parents and teachers). Most of the book is focused at this level as we discuss what happens in the classroom. However, children's lives are also significantly affected by the mesosystem, which includes interactions of microsystems such as how parents and teachers relate to each other. At a more distal level, the exosystem contains larger institutions such as public health, which impact how children are protected and treated during moments of crisis. The macrosystem and chronosystem involve the cultural values of how children are viewed and treated, and the historical context in which children happen to be born, respectively. Throughout the book, multiple systems will be relevant but consideration of the microsystem and the macrosystem will be especially critical. This is because classroom assessment occurs in the microsystem, but a *children's human rights approach* to assessment involves societal values and beliefs about children and their treatment. This perspective, then, puts us in the macrosystem. Although I will not continually mention these systems throughout the book, I do wish for these to be maintained in your minds as you consider the assessment of social and emotional wellbeing in children. I return to this idea at the very end of the book in Chapter 5.

Social and Emotional Assessment in the Context of Children's Rights: Three Principles

The three principles that form the basis of this book are shown as follows:

> **PRINCIPLE 1. There is little cognitive learning for children without social and emotional readiness and wellbeing. Some children need help acquiring the social and emotional competencies, attributes, and/or**

skills that will help them achieve a state of social and emotional readiness and wellbeing for learning.

PRINCIPLE 2. Social and emotional readiness and wellbeing can be formally or informally measured to yield data and inform interpretations about what is in the best interest of students. Students are rights holders in their own learning. These data can be used to facilitate children's acquisition of social and emotional competencies, attributes and/or skills in classrooms.

PRINCIPLE 3. Facilitating children's acquisition of social and emotional competencies, attributes and/or skills in the classroom requires earning children's trust. Trust comes about when teachers recognize and nurture their role as secondary attachment figures and as duty bearers in the lives of children.

These principles are not based on anecdotes and are not subject to the styles or whims of different teachers or researchers. The principles are simply necessary for children, and in fact, all human beings to learn. Those teachers who have worked with children for many years will appreciate the plainness of these principles. Some of you may not need or even wish to know about the empirical research that underlies these principles. However, knowing the relevant research literature matters. Knowing the research can be helpful – especially because it provides the evidence for explaining to others *what* you do in the classroom with the children you teach and *why* you do it. Moreover, these principles, when they are internalized into a teaching and assessment "mindset," can provide an extensive repertoire of ideas and resources for practice.

I will come back to these three principles repeatedly throughout this chapter and in the balance of this book. The aim is to show the growing empirical evidence for these three principles. With examples, moreover, you will see beyond the abstraction of the words and perceive the pattern or frame that emerges when these three principles work in concert. The pattern should inform a teacher's mindset for cultivating a learning environment wherein children's social and emotional competencies, attributes and/or skills are entrusted, measured and enriched to facilitate their learning.

Socio-Emotional Readiness and Wellbeing, Assessment and Pedagogical Alliances

Definition of Social and Emotional Readiness and Wellbeing

The first principle indicates that *there is little cognitive learning for children without social and emotional readiness and wellbeing.* I use the term social and emotional readiness and wellbeing instead of the usual *social-emotional learning* because the former term is more delimited than the latter. According to Weissberg, Durlak, Domitrovich, and Gullotta (2015, p. 6), social and emotional learning formally includes "competencies to understand and manage emotions, set and achieve positive goals, feel and show caring and concern for others, establish and maintain positive relationships, and make responsible decisions" (p. 6). However, Weissberg et al.'s use of the noun "learning" is too broad in scope given their definition. Learning can, technically, include the acquisition of positive and negative knowledge and skills. For example, children can *learn* to become excessively anxious during exam time. However, this is not a positive social and emotional learning outcome for many children. The substantive content of Weissberg et al.'s definition is intended to be positive and so is better aligned with the term "readiness and wellbeing" rather than "learning;" and, in fact, their definition is generally focused on helping the child become ready and well enough to learn.

At this juncture, a digression is needed. It involves acknowledging two legitimate concerns raised by Hoffman (2009) in her review of trends in social and emotional 'learning' in the United States. Both have an impact on the definition of children's social and emotional readiness and wellbeing. The first concern involves the emphasis on the *measurability* of social and emotional competencies. Emphasis on measurability involves issues of whether feasible and psychometrically reliable and valid tools can be developed to measure aspects of the *intended competencies*, for example, social collaboration or emotional regulation. Although measurability of constructs is typically considered a desirable feature to evaluate potential pedagogical interventions and their outcomes, the focus on measurability can eclipse some social and emotional competencies that are difficult to measure. For example, consider the experience of trust between teachers and students. Trust between students and teachers is a central experience in the creation of a nurturing learning environment, but it is difficult to measure. Indeed, some teachers may even eschew its measurement because of worries that students' evaluations may be unflattering (Leighton, 2021). The second concern of Hoffman (2009) involves a universalist assumption that *certain social and emotional competencies* are preferable over others. For example, competencies involving the management of emotions to keep calm and high levels of expression to show care for others may be preferred in North American cultures, but these may not be preferred in other cultures. Hence, the concern is that tools and criteria used to assess children's social and emotional competencies will not consider a breadth of culturally appropriate competencies for children. To this end, Hoffman (2009) has specifically critiqued the term social and emotional "learning" for its ambiguity and raised the question of what competencies or attributes[1] should fall under the scope of this type of "learning." Hoffman's (2009) critique is germane and consequential to the present discussion. Thus, I will come back to it repeatedly throughout the book. Notwithstanding Hoffman's critique, emphasizing ways to create caring and nurturing learning environments for children and exploring culturally appropriate measures of social and emotional competencies are desirable goals in my view.

Considering Weissberg et al.'s definition (2015) again, the competencies they delineate (i.e., understanding and managing emotions, setting and achieving positive goals, feeling and showing caring and concern for others, establishing and maintaining positive relationships, and making responsible decisions) should not be considered exhaustive or necessarily appropriate for all children. Other competencies could be added with varying levels of specificity given the children with which a teacher is working; for example, competencies to deescalate conflict, feel comfortable showing emotion, reflect on personal biases and express anger in constructive ways may be appropriate for some or all children.

Definitions are obviously useful to achieve a shared sense of understanding. However, the challenge with definitions is that the process of defining terms can create artificial boundaries. There is little doubt that we need to be precise about the social and emotional competencies being measured at any given time, but we must also acknowledge that specific social and emotional competencies are likely to be selected and specified for particular purposes. In other words, context is key in the teaching and assessment of these competencies.[2] A definition that is assumed to be applicable in all situations is not realistic or helpful to teachers or students. Depending on the needs of the student, the situation and the availability of specific tools, only then can particular social and emotional competencies be identified, defined, assessed and addressed specifically. Not everything that potentially falls under the umbrella term of social and emotional readiness and wellbeing may be measured nor relevant at one time. Thus, for the purpose of this book, I use the following conceptual definition of social and emotional readiness and wellbeing:

> **Social and emotional readiness and wellbeing consists of two inter-related processes. The first process is social and involves being part of a group of learners that collaborates for the purpose of achieving learning goals. This process requires students to acquire ways of behaving that allow them to advance their own learning without hindering the learning of others. The second process is emotional and involves developing a sense of awareness about how to use affect – both negative and positive – constructively to achieve desired learning goals. The operationalization of these processes depends on the specific situation and students of interest.**

Coming back to the first principle, then, the substance of it requires us to recognize that productive social and emotional competencies are not going to be the same for all students. Moreover, these competencies serve as a foundation for helping students find their own state of wellness and readiness to engage with classroom instruction and assessment. This first principle also implies that even the best content and curricular frameworks are not sufficient to enhance student academic performance if students lack the social and emotional readiness and wellness to interact with the instructional material. Some children may require training on distinct sides of a spectrum, such as to overcome debilitating shyness or anxiety, and others to "share the stage" or not be overly confident and disregard feedback. There also needs to be attention to the systemic social and emotional barriers that hinder student learning. Teachers must consider their own biases about how they perceive students' social and emotional competencies. For example, teachers who may perceive a female student as overly aggressive need to be sufficiently self-aware to question themselves about whether this perceived aggression is truly excessive or whether it is considered excessive only because of the student's female gender.

Students who experience social and emotional struggles often show an absence of adaptive competencies in the presence of maladaptive competencies (e.g., failing to express intentions [absence] and disrupting group projects [presence], ignoring teachers' exam instructions but excessively worrying about assessments, lacking empathy but hounding classmates, refusing to negotiate and exploding with anger). Competing social and emotional competencies often begin at an early age, with some children exhibiting internal distress involving lack of executive control (e.g., attention, planning, self-regulation), anger, anxiety and/or sadness. When left untreated, this distress can begin to interfere with their capability to adjust to learning environments. For example, in a study of 275 pre-school children, Denham and colleagues (2012) found that children who were clustered into a Social-Emotional Learning (SEL)-Risk group because of their scores on a variety of measures showed less knowledge of their emotions and opted for more angry-aggressive responses to imaginary scenarios than children who clustered into an SEL-Competent group.

Lacking knowledge of one's emotions or opting for angry or aggressive responses may not necessarily be maladaptive for individual children in impeccably controlled environments. However, this is rarely the case, and even if such environments did exist, they would not help prepare children for life's challenges. For example, lacking awareness of one's emotions often interferes with learning to attenuate maladaptive competencies and acquire adaptive competencies to reflect on challenges, listen to feedback, work with others, feel a sense of agency and importantly learn to do things differently. These are adaptive competencies that can help children navigate complex life circumstances. However, when children struggle socially and emotionally, they feel helpless, out of place, disengaged and desire an escape from what can become a noxious learning environment in the classroom.

Social and Emotional Assessment

The good news is that teachers do not have to guess students' social and emotional competencies. This is highlighted by the second principle: *Social and emotional readiness and wellbeing can be formally or informally measured to yield data and inform interpretations about what is in the best interest of students. Students are rights holders in their own learning. These data can be used to facilitate children's acquisition of social and emotional competencies, attributes and/or skills in classrooms.* For the purposes of this book, then, assessment is defined simply as the *appraisal or judgment of the nature, quality or ability of someone or something.* Assessments can be derived from formal or informal data. Formal data are gathered using standardized procedures (e.g., clinical interviews and surveys). Informal data are gathered using unstructured procedures (e.g., observations and conversations). Both types of data can serve assessment purposes with varying degrees of rigor.

Specifically, teachers can engage in five actions to acquire data or evidence to assess children's readiness and wellbeing for learning. The scope of these actions may begin informally and scale up to formal processes and tools as follows:

1. *Being attentive* to the students in the classroom in consistent ways to notice emerging patterns of maladaptive behavior such as students missing class, disengaging from activities,

fighting, isolating others and withdrawing from others. The simple act of being mindfully attentive to students is an informal, but powerful data gathering device that gives rise to increasingly more structured methods of gathering data for assessing students.

2. *Speaking with students*, one-on-one, to learn more about the origins and/or circumstances of maladaptive behavior. In most cases, teachers already do this reflexively. But what may not occur reflexively is the *documentation of these conversations and students' patterns* of maladaptive behavior. The act of documenting discussions with a student in a pedagogical journal begins to structure a typically informal process of data collection – discussions – into a more formal process. When entered into a journal immediately after the discussion occurs (i.e., a form of data capture), this process can guide reflection and future standardized procedures of data collection for assessment.

3. *Speaking with parents* to learn more about the origins and/ or circumstances of a child's home life is a relatively informal data collection device. However, discussions can reveal potentially relevant background variables to a student's struggles. If the discussion with parents is documented immediately after it occurs, then this process of data capture can guide reflection and future standardized procedures of data collection for assessment.

4. *Consulting with school counselors, psychologists* or nurses if a student's maladaptive behavior shows a pattern that is not resolved with one-on-one conversations between teachers and students. Consulting is another informal method of data collection as it presents another opportunity to delve deeper and learn about a student's situation. However, if the consultation is documented and leads to specific steps for working with the child and/or parents (e.g., a formal psychosocial assessment), then this represents a formal data collection process.

5. *Working with students individually or with an entire class to implement an intervention and gather formal data.* There are a variety of high-quality programs and tools that

are available for teachers to use in efforts to teach social and emotional competencies and assess children. The use of recognized programs and tools to assess the social and emotional "temperature" of all the students in class or a single student reflects a formal method of data collection. Depending on the specific tools that are implemented, the assessment may require a school psychologist or other professional to help with the interpretation of data.

Each of these five actions requires either a formal or an informal endeavor to gather data for assessment purposes. Formal data would typically originate from the administration of a proper psychological assessment where relevant and recognized tests are administered to the child, one-on-one, by a licensed professional to assess the child's cognitive, or social-emotional wellbeing (Leighton, 2019; McKown, 2015). These formal assessments are often necessary to diagnose and treat persistent and serious socio-emotional issues (e.g., Oppositional Defiant Disorder). However, formal data can also originate from programmatic surveys and experimental questionnaires that serve to assess intervention efforts.

The rigor of the tools that are used to gather data about students should correspond to the stakes associated with the assessments and decisions made about students (Assessment Work Group, 2019). For example, high-stakes assessments informing whether a child will be removed from a regular classroom and placed in a special education class should be accompanied by tools that have been systematically and empirically vetted for their appropriateness in informing these types of decisions. Typically, these tools are purchased and administered by professionals who have *qualification levels* B or C. Qualification levels are designed to distinguish the level of training required to administer tools and interpret resulting data. For example, qualification B is required to administer the Behavior Assessment for Children, Third Edition (BASC-3; Reynolds & Kamphaus, 2015). The BASC-3 provides a comprehensive measure of children's behavior and emotions from Preschool to Grade 11 and includes scales for the teacher, parent and child to complete.

Alternatively, relatively low-stakes assessments, such as discussing a child's test anxiety with parents, can be triggered by a teacher's repeated observation and/or use of experimental self-report questionnaires that allow the teacher to gather preliminary data about the child's state of wellness. For example, the *Spence Children's Anxiety Scale* (SCAS; Spence, 1997, 1998; see also Holly, Little, Pina & Caterino, 2015) is free of charge and can be administered by non-psychologists. According to Holly et al. (2015), the SCAS is a 45-item self-report tool designed to provide information on several forms of anxiety (e.g., generalized, separation, social). The SCAS was normed in Australia with children 8–15 years of age, shows sensitivity to interventions designed to reduce anxiety in children, and has been translated into many languages. Items include situational statements designed to probe potential worry and fear in students as follows:

- I worry about things.
- I feel scared when I have to take a test.
- I worry about being away from my parents.
- I suddenly feel as if I can't breathe when there is no reason for this.

Children who indicate high agreement with many of these types of statements may be reflecting a form of maladaptive anxiety that interferes with feeling ready and sufficiently well to learn in the classroom. The normative data to interpret children's scores can be obtained from Susan Spence's website. A formal interpretation of scores may require the assistance of a professional psychologist to assess how individual children compare to the normative sample. In the absence of a formal interpretation, however, a teacher can discuss the reasons for the worries of a child who is found to agree with several of these items.

The SCAS can be used free of charge and downloaded from Susan Spence's website at https://www.scaswebsite.com/1_1_.html. The SCAS has been identified as experimental and appropriate for use in community screening and prevention, as well as research (Spence, Barrett, & Turner, 2003). Although an overview of the scale indicates that it is "intended for research or for clinical use under the supervision and care of a trained mental health clinician" (n.p. https://www.scaswebsite.com/1_1_.html), a teacher can administer this scale with the assistance from a school counselor to assess children who may be at-risk for anxiety in the classroom. In fact, these types of instruments can become part of a teacher's toolbox in attending to the social and emotional aspects of the classroom. I discuss additional tools and, importantly, a framework for guiding the responsible use and interpretation of these measurement tools in the sections that follow and in subsequent chapters of the book. For now, the important take-away message is that good tools can be found free of charge to help teachers learn more about children's social and emotional competencies.

Another example of an experimental tool that can be used to gather evidence about students' social and emotional readiness and wellbeing is the 26-item *Attitudes Towards Mistakes Inventory* (ATMI; Leighton, Guo & Tang, 2021). Although the tool was originally developed and validated to assess the attitudes of postsecondary students, the wording of the items was modified to be used with elementary school students. Figure 1.2 shows items from the short version of the ATMI for elementary school students. Data from studies with children aged 6–11 show that the ATMI is a useful tool to initiate conversations about the way in which students report viewing, feeling and behaving about the mistakes they make in learning situations. Assessing students' attitudes towards mistakes can be helpful for students to identify and talk about common fears in learning environments and feedback conversations. For example, if students have strong feelings about disappointing teachers when they make mistakes, these feelings can lead to avoidant behavior (e.g., not wanting to participate in challenging assignments, not wanting to present publicly, not engaging with feedback).

Assessing children's views on their mistakes builds on Carol Dweck's research on mindsets for learning (Dweck, 2017). Many readers will be familiar with the decades of research Dweck has conducted with her colleagues showing that children (and adults) who view their mistakes as arising from effort and

Section 2 Mistakes	Agree	Not Sure	Disagree
1. I feel bad when I don't know the answer to a question.	👍	✋	👎
2. I feel smart when I don't make mistakes.	👍	✋	👎
3. Sometimes I feel my friends are smarter than I am.	👍	✋	👎
4. I work hard at school to never make mistakes.	👍	✋	👎
5. I like to learn things that are easy.	👍	✋	👎
6. I feel I let my teacher down when I make mistakes.	👍	✋	👎
7. I try to be perfect in everything I do.	👍	✋	👎

Figure 1.2 Revised Short-Form of the ATMI (Children's Version). License owned by Author.

learned skills are much more engaged in learning than students who view their mistakes as arising from immutable intelligence (for a summary of this work, see Dweck, 2017; Dweck & Yeager, 2019). Although Dweck's research has led to school-based materials and proprietary curricular programs that teachers and schools can purchase (see mindsetworks.com), these for-purchase tools are not always needed to implement the kernel of her ideas. The beauty of Dweck's fundamental research is that it helps us to recognize that children's basic underlying beliefs serve to demotivate children in learning situations. Thus, there are alternate ways, aside from using proprietary curricular programs, to help children recognize and work to overcome debilitating beliefs about themselves as learners. For example, feedback conversations between teachers and students that emphasize effort and focus specifically on improving skills can help students apprehend how they are capable of improving their performance.

Regardless of the data gathered, the data should be used in a way to help teachers and other professionals generate evidence-based conclusions about students' social and emotional readiness and wellbeing for learning. Gathering these data can serve a preventative function in helping to identify children who exhibit maladaptive competencies and correct these competencies to avoid serious obstacles later in children's schooling, especially as more challenging learning situations emerge. However, to obtain useful data of any kind from a child, the child needs to be able to trust the teacher's motives and the course of action that ensues from the assessment. In the next section, attachment and the pedagogical alliance between students and teachers are presented.

Building Socio-emotional Readiness and Wellbeing: Attachment and the Pedagogical Alliance

As front-line professionals working with children, teachers serve key roles in students' social and emotional lives (Leighton, Guo, Chu, & Tang, 2018). As indicated in principle 3, teachers can *facilitate children's acquisition of social and emotional competencies, attributes and/or skills by earning children's trust. Trust comes about when teachers recognize and nurture their role as secondary attachment figures and duty bearers in the lives of children.* In this section, I elaborate on how teachers serve as secondary attachment figures and then in the final section, how teachers serve as duty bearers in the protection of children's rights to learn.

Teachers are some of the first adults (aside from primary caregivers) to have regular time and opportunity to observe children's systematic struggles with social and emotional readiness and wellness for learning. For example, teachers are the ones who have opportunity to observe if children routinely show up late to class, are ill-prepared, spend most of their time by themselves and appear withdrawn, and/or are the object of teasing or ridicule from other students. Because teachers spend so much time with groups of children within a given academic year, they are in a privileged position to notice, assess and affect social and emotional change for students within their classrooms.

Good teachers take leadership in creating intentionally caring *learning environments* for the students they teach. This environment involves not only curricular matters but also matters of psychological wellness. The learning environment is a result of the collection of behaviors that teachers make every day depending on their confidence and experience with children – how to physically seat students, how to begin a class, how to respond to and comfort individual students, how to respect children's views and ideas, how to organize a lesson plan, how to introduce curricular initiatives. The learning environment is set up to either support students' social and emotional readiness and wellbeing or, sadly, to overlook the potentially harmful effects that poorly envisioned learning environments can have on the students being served. In the next few paragraphs, I explain the importance of the student-teacher relationship or *pedagogical alliance* (Leighton et al., 2018) for the assessment of students' social and emotional readiness and wellbeing. To lay the groundwork for describing the pedagogical alliance, it is necessary to first introduce the psychological concept of *attachment*. Given the centrality of attachment processes in a child's life, I will go into some depth into what attachment means, how it has been traditionally measured and the mechanism by which it is believed to influence human development and learning. Notwithstanding, a comprehensive treatment is beyond the scope of this book, and the interested reader should consult several excellent books on the topic such as Goldberg's (2000) *Attachment and Development* and Duschinsky's (2020) *Cornerstones of Attachment Research*.

Attachment refers to the way individuals typically respond and form relationships to other human beings (Pianta, 2016; Sroufe, 2021). Early in a child's life, attachment *figures* are those adults who take care of the child and introduce the child to basic contingencies in social relations such as receiving help when one asks for help. In other words, attachment figures are the very first people in the child's life who introduce the child to the experience of feeling safe in one's social environment or, alternatively, in peril. The healthiness of attachment is determined by a child's biological characteristics and the nature of the environment in which the child lives. Two central environmental variables are the *actual* support and *consistency* of the support children can expect from adults charged with protecting them. Parents and/or caregivers are considered primary attachment figures in a child's life.

The cognitive mechanism by which attachment is assumed to exert its influence on the child is through the *internal working model*. The internal working model serves as a type of filter or lens through which the child interprets and understands his or her social environment. As shown in Figure 1.3, the internal working model filters or frames all social and emotional information coming in from the environment to help the child make decisions about how to regulate distress; for example, a young child who sees her mother leaving a room and immediately feels distraught might soothe herself by thinking '*she is coming right back.*' For those readers who are familiar with concepts such as schemas, frames and mental models, the internal working model is similar in function but specifically focused on social and emotional matters pertaining to human relationships. The internal working model, therefore, is a representational structure that serves to *store* propositional knowledge of what the child experiences socially and emotionally with others and then to *guide* actions for reducing stress. For example, a parent who is erratic in how consistently he or she soothes a child's grief assists in the creation of an internal working model wherein adults are unreliable and therefore lacking in utility for the child. The basic function of attachment is shown in Figure 1.3.

Building on Figure 1.3, Figure 1.4 outlines some of the most basic influences in the development of attachment (Cassidy, Jones, & Shaver, 2013). Figure 1.4 is a basic model, and it should be noted that a full illustration of attachment processes would require several more variables, including the child's biological temperament, and additional environmental variables such as the level of home adversity experienced by the family

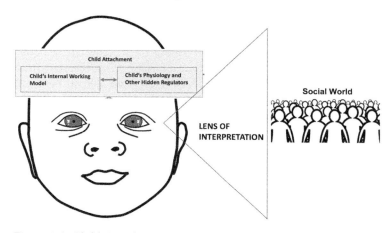

Figure 1.3 Child Attachment Functions as a Lens for Interpreting the Social World. License owned by Author.

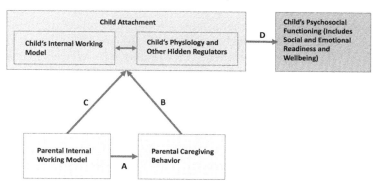

Figure 1.4   Basic Model of Attachment Processes Created by Author Based on Cassidy et al.'s (2013) Description. License owned by Author.

unit, socioeconomic status, education, health and cultural factors (see Cassidy et al., 2013).

The concept of attachment originated in the 1950s with the research of John Bowlby and Mary Ainsworth. From observations of the effects of early loss and deprivation on human development, they proposed attachment theory (Bretherton, 1992).

Unbeknownst to both at the time, Bowlby and Ainsworth had identified one of the most foundational socio-emotional concepts to underlie human functioning – the experience of being securely connected to central members of one's social group. It is difficult to overstate the influence of attachment in how human beings develop in learning environments:

> The Bowlby/Ainsworth attachment theory was one of the most significant advances in psychology in the second half of the 20th century. The outpouring of research on attachment has had a major impact both within and outside of academia. It has pervaded the domains not only of developmental psychology but also clinical psychology, social psychology, psychiatry and social work.
>
> (Sroufe, 2021, p. 1)

Children's attachment is measured by observing their behavioral patterns in how they seek adult attention, assistance and subsequently respond following periods of distress. The well-known research procedure for measuring variability in infant attachment is the *Strange Situation*, devised by Mary Ainsworth (Ainsworth & Bell, 1970). In temporal order, there are eight basic events or episodes to the Strange Situation as shown in Figure 1.5. If the child shows any inconsolable distress during any one of these episodes, the procedure is terminated.

As can be seen in Figure 1.5, the initial episodes set the stage for the fifth and eighth episodes. The fifth and eighth episodes are crucial for eliciting the focal behaviors from the child in the measurement of attachment. For example, in the fifth episode, when the mother returns, this "reunion" is central to evoking the child's response to the parent and indirectly evaluating the child's attachment. Depending on the reunion between mother and child, Ainsworth identified three categories of attachment:

1. *Secure Attachment*. The child appears to trust the parent. The child is observed to explore the toys freely during episode 1 while the mother is sitting. As soon as the child notices the mother has left in episodes 3 and 6, the child becomes distressed. However, the child is observed to be

Episode 1	The mother and child enter a room with the investigator and then the investigator leaves.
Episode 2	While mother sits in a chair, the child is allowed to explore the available toys. The mother participates in the exploration only if the child seeks her attention.
Episode 3	A stranger enters the room, sits quietly in the room, then chats with the mother, and then slowly approaches child to show the child a toy. Discreetly, the mother leaves at this point.
Episode 4	The stranger shows child the toy if the child shows interest in the new toy, otherwise the stranger simply watches the child play if the child is busy with the existing toys. If the child appears distressed, the stranger attempts to comfort or distract child. This last about 3 minutes.
Episode 5	The mother enters the room again and waits at the door to see the child's response. Now the stranger leaves the room.
Episode 6	Once the child has re-established contact with mother, the mother leaves again but this time before she leaves she says good-bye to the child. The child is left alone in the room.
Episode 7	The stranger enters the room and attempts to play with the child as previously done.
Episode 8	The mother returns again, the stranger leaves, and the reunion between mother and child is observed.

Figure 1.5   The Basic Content of the Eight Episodes in the Strange Situation. License owned by Author.

quickly comforted when the mother returns in episodes 5 and 8. The mother is observed to show consistent emotional warmth and expression towards the child. The child goes back to exploring the environment once again.

2. *Insecure Avoidant.* The child appears to distrust the parent. Although the child explores the toys freely during episode 1 while the mother is sitting, the child does not show much distress when the child notices the mother has left in episodes 3 and 6. Moreover, when the mother returns in episodes 5 and 8, the child does not seek her for comfort. The mother is observed to consistently lack warmth and emotional expression towards the child. The child continues to explore the environment.

3. *Insecure Ambivalent.* The child appears to distrust the parent. The child shows hesitancy in exploring the toys during episode 1 while the mother is sitting. As soon as the child notices the mother has left in episodes 3 and 6, the child shows signs of distress. When the mother returns in episodes 5 and 8, the child seeks her out and shows anger, clinginess and resistance to being with the mother. The caregiver shows inconsistency in the emotion expressed towards the

child; for example, the mother alternates between showing warmth, coldness and even despair in comforting the child. The latter response tends to exacerbate the child's originally distressed response (Benoit, 2004). The child is observed to not re-establish wellness quickly or easily.

The three categories of attachment reflect a continuum of response to a parent's warmth and consistency. Securely attached children are inferred to trust caregivers to soothe them during distress because they consistently seek them out and then, subsequently, demonstrate relief. Insecure-avoidant children are inferred to distrust caregivers to soothe them because they consistently avoid the parent as a source of relief from distress. Insecure-ambivalent children are also inferred to distrust caregivers but for different reasons as insecure avoidant children. Insecure ambivalent children are inferred to distrust caregivers because the parent is viewed as unreliable in responding to the child's distress.

The attachment behavior of most children is predictable and can be assigned into one of these three categories. According to Howe (2005; Brown & Ward, 2013), for example, about 50–55% of non-clinical populations exhibit secure attachment, 20–25% exhibit insecure-avoidant attachment and approximately 10% exhibit insecure-ambivalent attachment. Another 15% of the non-clinical population show what is called a *disorganized style* of attachment, which was added to account for a proportion of children who did not show any consistent pattern in how they responded to the caregiver during the reunion. Kids categorized as showing a disorganized attachment style sometimes exhibit trusting behavior towards the parent and at other times appear to disregard or completely mistrust the parent. According to Benoit (2004), the disorganized style has been found to emerge when caregivers exhibit *atypical and erratic responses* towards the child that frighten the child. The atypicality of the parental response is not simple disregard or grief but, rather extreme, inconsistent and often disconnected from reality. For example, in response to a child's call for comfort, the parent may respond with excessive consolation, violence or sexual behaviors towards the child. One of the most psychologically damaging aspects of the social and emotional environment that breeds a disorganized attachment style in children is chaotic behaviors from the parent – so much so that it prevents the child from developing a reliable internal working model for dealing with distress and planning for protection. Not surprisingly, this attachment style is disproportionately represented in samples of children who exhibit psychopathology in later functioning (Green & Goldwyn, 2002; Van IJzendoorn, Schuengel, & Bakermans-Kranenburg, 1999).

The psychological research linking children's attachment to physical, cognitive, social and emotional outcomes has been robust (Cassidy et al., 2013; Sroufe, 2021). The quality of children's early attachment predicts whether children will grow to be confident in interactions with other human beings or detached, disengaged, distrustful and/or chronically anxious (Cassidy et al., 2013). For example, in a recent meta-analysis of empirical studies, Spruit et al. (2020) showed that a child's early attachment predicted the internalizing disorder of depression in childhood and adolescence. This meta-analysis is significant because much of the early research had tied insecure attachment mainly to externalizing disorders such as addictive behaviors, rule-breaking, aggression, inattention and impulsivity (Cassidy et al., 2013; Kimonis & Frick, 2016). However, Spruit et al.'s research shows that insecure attachment predicts long-term internal distress as well.

The link between children's attachment and their social-emotional readiness and wellbeing for learning is significant. First, children who show secure attachment to primary caregivers have been found to perform better academically, demonstrate better cognitive skills and executive functions than those who show insecure attachment (Cassidy et al., 2013). This means that attachment matters greatly to how well students are poised to learn in the classroom. Second, insecure attachment is reliably associated with internalizing disorders such as depression in both children and adolescents (Spruit et al., 2020), as well as externalizing disorders (Muris, Meesters, & van den Berg, 2003; Roelofs, Meesters, ter Huurne, Bamelis, & Muris, 2006). Both internalizing and externalizing disorders are associated with lower academic outcomes in students. Again, this matters greatly to how well students are poised to learn in the classroom. Third, positive student-teacher relationships can ameliorate some of the negative effects of internalizing and externalizing disorders (Aldrup, Klusmann, & Lüdtke, 2020; Forster, Gower, Borowsky, & McMorris, 2017), and help improve students' overall health outcomes into adulthood (Kim, 2021). For example, in a study of over 100,000 adolescents in grades 8, 9 and 11, Forster et al. (2017) found that positive student-teacher relationships buffered the association between children's multiple adverse home experiences and their tendency to use prescription medication for *non-medical* purposes. This again matters greatly because it shows that teachers can help attenuate children's distress.

Teachers can help attenuate or lower children's distress because teachers serve as *secondary* attachment figures in the lives of children; children look to teachers, as expert authority figures, for protection and comfort in moments of hardship (Leighton, Seitz, Chu, & Gomez Bustos, 2016; Pianta, 2016). When teachers enter into meaningful relationships with the students they teach, I call these relationships *pedagogical alliances*. The relationship between students and teachers is critical because teachers oversee the vital process of learning for students at a time when students are most vulnerable, young and impressionable. Consider that teachers often see the same group of children *daily* for an academic year. During this time, teachers have authority and *power* to make and administer rules, judge student behavior and assign grades, and set a learning climate in the classroom they teach. Teachers set a tone in the classroom; some teachers are known for their meticulous classroom organization and some teachers are known to be fun and easy going. Not surprisingly, then, students come to admire and even feel life-changing motivation as a result of interactions with some teachers. Conversely, some students come to fear and even feel repulsed by their interactions with other teachers. There is no doubt that teachers can arouse strong emotional reactions in students as one would expect in any significant human relationship with elements of unequal power.

According to Robert Pianta (e.g., 1992a, 1992b, 2016; Hafen et al., 2012), a developmental psychologist who has spent his professional life conducting empirical research on teacher-student relationships, it is not happenstance that teachers play a foundational instructional role in the social and emotional well-being of students. Teachers play this foundational role precisely because teachers serve as attachment figures for students – albeit *secondary attachment figures*. The proposal to think of teachers as secondary attachment figures is not done casually. It is proposed specifically because it helps us understand why teachers have the influence they do on the children they teach (Allen, Pianta, Gregory, Mikami, & Lun, 2011; Pianta, Belsky, Vandergrift, Houts, & Morrison, 2008). By understanding the power that teachers have over children they teach in the course of an academic year, we can begin to appreciate the role and responsibility teachers inherit in shaping the social and emotional lives of children, and by association, their academic performance. Like parents, teachers are in positions of authority over children. In most jurisdictions, children are required by law to attend school. Thus, what teachers do with this authority during the extensive amount of time spent with a child during the formative years of schooling is believed to influence major aspects of the child's internal working model. For example, teachers can use their authority to help or hinder the child during times of academic distress in predictable ways. Some teachers may knowingly or unknowingly devote more attention to 'favorite' students while providing less to 'troublemakers.' Given the positions of influence teachers occupy in the classroom, teachers can be expected to affect basic aspects of children's internal working models about the safety of learning environments. Adult attachment figures, then, are key players in children's social and emotional functioning by instantiating behaviors that shape a child's trust in being helped if help is needed. Thus, what teachers do or not do in the classroom to affect children's learning becomes a critical topic of analysis and study. It becomes a topic of interest in the service of children's rights.

Programmatic interventions and resources used by teachers (and schools) serve to operationalize the ways in which children's social and emotional competencies are defined, shaped and assessed in classrooms. Toward this end, there are many excellent repositories of resources for teachers to use in the operationalization of social and emotional readiness and wellbeing. Three evidence-based repositories are the (1) *Collaborative for Academic, Social and Emotional Learning* (CASEL) (casel.org), (2) *XSEL Labs* (xsel-labs.com/), and (3) *Teachstone* (teachstone.com). Each of these web-based repositories provides access to theoretical orientation materials, research findings about programs, reports and evidence-based tools. These resources are helpful in assisting teachers to not just learn about children's social and emotional competencies but also design learning environments where cognitive skills are taught against a context of social and emotional wellness. Depending on the resources chosen, assessment tools and formats will guide what is observed, measured and discussed with children as part of the learning process.

The challenge with using any one approach, however, is falling into the trap of believing that it is the one and single approach to use with all students. As Hoffman (2009) cautions, social and emotional competencies should be tailored to the unique needs of the child. The assessment of social and emotional competencies, of which a child's readiness to learn and wellbeing are a core part, will often involve using a variety of measurement tools and techniques (McKown, 2019). In fact, an explicit recognition that there is no *one size fits all* is part of the mindset that teachers need to acquire and bring to the learning environment. A reliance on available survey tools and rating checklists cannot relieve the responsibility of teachers to question the assumptions and appropriateness of different resources for advancing the social and emotional interests of children in culturally appropriate ways. The preparation that schools and teachers develop in using these learning and assessment resources is therefore crucial for their proper implementation. This is underscored in the 2013 CASEL guide where it states (Durlak, Weissberg, Dymnicki, Taylor, & Schellinger, 2011):

> the quality of program implementation is… a function of how prepared schools are when they adopt an SEL program, the extent to which all

staff members are involved in that decision, and whether or not there is real commitment to training and implementation support. When districts and schools support high-quality program implementation, the impact of SEL programs is significantly strengthened.

(p. 3)

There is little doubt that an overall commitment to the proper use of these resources is necessary. However, despite the evidentiary strength of some of the resources, in my view there is something fundamentally missing – namely, an explicit ethical framework for how children are to be viewed and treated in the learning environment. The justification for improving children's social and emotional readiness and wellness should be broader than simply to enhance children's *academic success* (Hoffman, 2009). If the justification of children's social and emotional readiness and wellness is understood to be largely about academic success, the process becomes largely transactional and ironically fails to recognize the inherent wholeness of children irrespective of their academic prowess. Realistically, not all children can or will meet pre-specified academic targets given distinct proclivities, but they still deserve healthfulness in the learning environments they inhabit. Thus, there needs to be insight and flexibility in the assessment tools and in the criteria used to assess the efficacy of the efforts to teach social and emotional competencies. In other words, a broader set of humanistic goals should be identified for the particular needs of the students involved.

In the implementation of programs to teach social and emotional competencies, the assessments used are probably the most contentious aspect of the program. Any kind of assessment is high stakes for the person being assessed if the assessor uses the information to make a formal decision that affects one's wellbeing. The decision or conclusion does not have to be explicit. It can be implicit and outside of the assessor's awareness. If the assessor has power, even implicit judgments can be used to benefit or disadvantage the individual assessed. Judgments are rarely neutral. For example, teachers might talk to their students casually at the beginning of the school year and from that point on begin to form impressions about students' character, abilities and motivations. Even benign interactions can have implicit repercussions in terms of student-teacher attention and opportunity for student advancement. This is probably one reason why assessments can be more politically controversial than any other aspect of the curriculum among teachers, parents and students. Not surprisingly, then, when schools and teachers venture into the teaching and *assessment* of social and emotional competencies, it raises the specter of what will be done with the assessment results. Questions of why certain competencies are being taught and not others, and what explicit judgments will be made about the children involved are obvious ones to ask. Less obvious questions are those that pertain to the implicit consequences of those explicit judgments about the child. For example, the question of how teachers and other school officials might support or *attempt to modify* student behavior based on assessment results is much less obvious.

We need to recognize that, unlike curricular subjects like Language Arts and Math, a child's social and emotional competencies are not aspects of a child that can be fit into some institutionally mandated "performance standard," where correct and incorrect ways of thinking and acting can be imposed from a majority perspective. Social and emotional competencies are less dependent on a given curriculum and much more dependent on a child's temperament, family and/or culture (Calkins, 2007; Hecht & Shin, 2015). For example, certain social and emotional competencies, such as peer collaboration and agreeableness, may be less appealing or even difficult to acquire for some children with very high abilities (Preckel, Baudson, Krolak-Schwerdt & Glock, 2015). Consequently, the assessment of social and emotional competencies needs to be conducted within a context that not only provides a theoretical and evidentiary grounding for tools, but also an explicitly ethical backdrop for their use and interpretation.

I propose that an ethical focus on the teaching and assessment of children's social and emotional competencies requires *revitalizing* a deep understanding of *the child as a developing person* beyond the particulars of academic achievement (Rogers,

1969). Subject to this understanding, the teaching and assessment of social and emotional competencies needs to be conducted within a context that acknowledges the uniqueness of human beings, their dignity and their rights to wellness. It is for this reason that the United Nations Convention on the Rights of the Child (CRC) should be included in the context of all classroom instruction and assessment but especially as it pertains to children's social and emotional wellness. The teaching and assessment of social and emotional competencies provides an opportunity to recognize teachers as duty bearers and children as rights holders; specifically, children have explicit inalienable rights in the classroom as human beings and irrespective of any assessment outcomes.

The United Nations Convention on the Rights of the Child: Teachers as Duty Bearers

The CRC is a 54-article agreement that was adopted in 1989 by the United Nations. The full text is publicly available and can be found at the site of the Office of the High Commissioner (www.ohchr.org/en/professionalinterest/pages/crc.aspx). A children-friendly version of the CRC is also publicly available and can be found at the UNICEF site (www.unicef.org/sop/convention-rights-child-child-friendly-version). One hundred and ninety-six State Parties (countries) have ratified the CRC agreement with the sole exception of the United States. Parties that have ratified the agreement are bound to it by international law. The United States has signed but not ratified the agreement. This means that although it is not bound by it, the United States cannot act in opposition to it. In practice, however, this is unenforceable.

The 54 articles of the CRC can be grouped into four categories of basic human rights for children:

1.   Protection from abuse, exploitation and harm;
2.   Provision of health care, education and an acceptable standard of living;

3. Participation in the form of being heard and having a voice in matters involving the child with respect to their advancing capacities; and
4. Specific protection and provisions for traditionally vulnerable populations such as racialized children, Indigenous children and children with disabilities.

Although all four categories can be applied to what happens to children in the classroom and at school, the categories are especially germane to the teaching and assessment of social and emotional competencies. Category 3 is perhaps most relevant. According to category 3, all children should be given the opportunity to voice their impressions and ideas about what they are being asked to do in the name of learning and about the judgments that are made about them from assessment results. Category 4 is the next relevant category. It emphasizes the need to be extra vigilant in the treatment of particular groups of children, some of whom have been historically disadvantaged in many classroom and school settings. For example, many Indigenous children in Canadian schools have been subjected to maltreatment and this continues to this day in some classrooms (Directions Evidence and Policy Research Group, 2016).

Although the CRC is not the first human rights treaty in which children are included, it is the one that meticulously outlines the intersection of children's rights in a variety of domains. This makes the CRC uniquely relevant in the teaching and assessment of social and emotional competencies. David (2002) elucidates this uniqueness:

> The Convention is unique among the seven major international human rights treaties as it groups comprehensively civil and political rights with economic, social and cultural ones. It strongly re-affirms the indivisibility and interdependence of all rights and suggests a holistic vision of the child (Committee on the Rights of the Child 1996). This has far-reaching implications for states as the Convention implies improved and stronger interaction between various departments and ministries (such as ministries of social affairs, the family,

health, education, justice, labour, the interior, defence, finance etc.) and related measures.

(p. 260)

Often when educators and parents initially hear about the CRC, they assume it mostly includes a listing of children's rights in relation to children's protection from abuse, exploitation and harm (category 1). Although these rights are obviously included, what makes the CRC distinctive is the inclusion of children's *civil rights to participation* (category 2) (David, 2002). Essentially, these are the rights that give children a voice or, more broadly, freedom of expression. Rights to participation imply that the child should be party to decisions about what is happening to the child. The CRC positions the child as a highly relevant source of information about what the child feels, experiences and thinks about the activities of the classroom. Children's rights to participation are elaborated in several articles of the CRC (i.e., 12, 13, 14, 15, 16 and 17). Given their significance to the present chapter, these six articles are reproduced in full in Figure 1.6.

Primary Implication of Children's Rights for Teachers

There are several reasons for using the CRC as an explicit ethical framework for how children are to be viewed and treated in the learning environment, including in the implementation of social and emotional programs and assessments. As mentioned previously, the CRC provides a broad humanistic perspective on the *child as a developing person*. This is a perspective or mindset that a teacher ought to have in order to serve the best interests of the child in the classroom, especially in relation to teaching and assessing the child in how to think, feel and act. Although there are specific implications of the CRC for the teaching and assessment of social and emotional competencies, one of the primary implications of the CRC for teachers pertains to reminding them of their role as *duty bearers*.

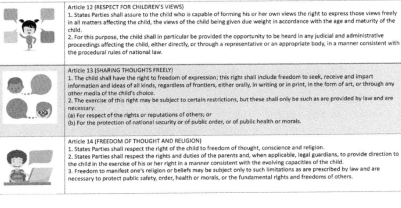

	Article 12 (RESPECT FOR CHILDREN'S VIEWS) 1. States Parties shall assure to the child who is capable of forming his or her own views the right to express those views freely in all matters affecting the child, the views of the child being given due weight in accordance with the age and maturity of the child. 2. For this purpose, the child shall in particular be provided the opportunity to be heard in any judicial and administrative proceedings affecting the child, either directly, or through a representative or an appropriate body, in a manner consistent with the procedural rules of national law.
	Article 13 (SHARING THOUGHTS FREELY) 1. The child shall have the right to freedom of expression; this right shall include freedom to seek, receive and impart information and ideas of all kinds, regardless of frontiers, either orally, in writing or in print, in the form of art, or through any other media of the child's choice. 2. The exercise of this right may be subject to certain restrictions, but these shall only be such as are provided by law and are necessary: (a) For respect of the rights or reputations of others; or (b) For the protection of national security or of public order, or of public health or morals.
	Article 14 (FREEDOM OF THOUGHT AND RELIGION) 1. States Parties shall respect the right of the child to freedom of thought, conscience and religion. 2. States Parties shall respect the rights and duties of the parents and, when applicable, legal guardians, to provide direction to the child in the exercise of his or her right in a manner consistent with the evolving capacities of the child. 3. Freedom to manifest one's religion or beliefs may be subject only to such limitations as are prescribed by law and are necessary to protect public safety, order, health or morals, or the fundamental rights and freedoms of others.

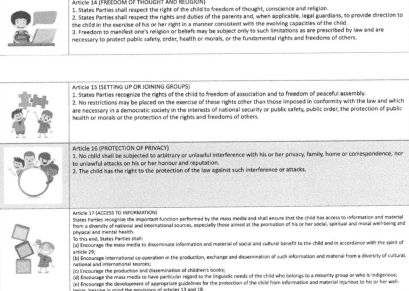

	Article 15 (SETTING UP OR JOINING GROUPS) 1. States Parties recognize the rights of the child to freedom of association and to freedom of peaceful assembly. 2. No restrictions may be placed on the exercise of these rights other than those imposed in conformity with the law and which are necessary in a democratic society in the interests of national security or public safety, public order, the protection of public health or morals or the protection of the rights and freedoms of others.
	Article 16 (PROTECTION OF PRIVACY) 1. No child shall be subjected to arbitrary or unlawful interference with his or her privacy, family, home or correspondence, nor to unlawful attacks on his or her honour and reputation. 2. The child has the right to the protection of the law against such interference or attacks.
	Article 17 (ACCESS TO INFORMATION) States Parties recognize the important function performed by the mass media and shall ensure that the child has access to information and material from a diversity of national and international sources, especially those aimed at the promotion of his or her social, spiritual and moral well-being and physical and mental health. To this end, States Parties shall: (a) Encourage the mass media to disseminate information and material of social and cultural benefit to the child and in accordance with the spirit of article 29; (b) Encourage international co-operation in the production, exchange and dissemination of such information and material from a diversity of cultural, national and international sources; (c) Encourage the production and dissemination of children's books; (d) Encourage the mass media to have particular regard to the linguistic needs of the child who belongs to a minority group or who is indigenous; (e) Encourage the development of appropriate guidelines for the protection of the child from information and material injurious to his or her well-being, bearing in mind the provisions of articles 13 and 18.

Figure 1.6 Six of the 54 Articles of the CRC. Images by Kidaha at Pixabay. com is licensed under CC BY 4.0.

The Teacher as Duty Bearer and the Child as Rights Holder

By virtue of their professional training and certification, it is evident that teachers must assume a responsibility to the children they teach. If they do not, their employment is unlikely to continue for long! The professional responsibility teachers assume most often involves the roles of *mentor* and *assessor*. Teachers are expected to have training in pedagogy, know a jurisdiction's program of studies (curriculum), deliver lessons in expert manner, manage classroom activities, assess student understanding and help students improve their acquisition of knowledge and skills.

According to the CRC, however, teachers' responsibility also encompasses another role, namely, that of *duty bearer*. Duty bearers are persons or entities that are obligated to follow the terms of a ratified treaty. In the case of the CRC, persons who have relevant responsibilities in their work with children serve as duty bearers in applying the provisions of the CRC. For example, teachers, pediatricians, nurses and social workers are all duty bearers. The obligations that a teacher has as a duty bearer can dovetail with the professional responsibility that a teacher assumes as mentor and assessor but the two are not the same. One difference is the underlying scope of accountability towards children associated with being a duty bearer versus being a professionally responsible teacher. For example, consider the following two scenarios: (1) A teacher employs a social and emotional initiative in the classroom because the teacher is following the programmatic direction of the school principal and/or the district. (2) A teacher explores social and emotional teaching and assessment strategies because the teacher is protecting, providing and promoting children's wellbeing in the classroom irrespective of any formal program at the school and/or district level. In the first scenario, the teacher complies with the social and emotional program as part of professional responsibility. In the second scenario, the teacher is not simply complying but actively searching for ways in which to support children's wellbeing irrespective of any explicit direction the school might afford. Although it is expected that teachers will comply with a school's programmatic directions, complying does not mean embracing or internalizing the reasons for such an approach. In contrast, in the second scenario, the teacher is doing more than complying. Instead, the teacher shows an inherent commitment to children's overall wellbeing, a commitment that is unlikely to change or terminate with variations at the administrative level.

The perspective of the *child as a developing person* who necessitates protection, provision and promotion as per the CRC can serve to safeguard children as rights holders in social and emotional learning and assessment initiatives. This perspective is necessary to balance the codified viewpoints that originate from professional teaching organizations but include little about the explicit protection, provision and promotion of children. For instance, in the province of Alberta, the Alberta Teacher's Association (ATA, 2021a) publishes a code of professional conduct for member teachers that includes guidance on the relation teachers should have with pupils, colleagues, school authorities and the profession. The guidance on teacher's conduct towards pupils contains seven points and begins with a clear statement about the dignity and rights of all persons:

The teacher teaches in a manner that respects the dignity and rights of all persons without prejudice as to race, religious beliefs, colour, gender, sexual orientation, gender identity, gender expression, physical characteristics, disability, marital status, family status, age, ancestry, place of origin, place of residence, socioeconomic background or linguistic background.

(p. 1)

Many teacher professional organizations have similar types of statements. However, you will notice that this statement focuses on the teacher and the teaching but not the student. Nowhere in this statement or in the broader document or in the related *Teachers' Rights and Responsibilities* (ATA, 2021b) is there mention of whether children have any specific rights in the classroom.

However, the child's perspective matters; their voice and the freedom to express their thoughts. The perspective of the child as a developing person needs to be at the fore of teachers' efforts to shape the child's thoughts, feelings and actions. Much like the view individuals assume when looking at a perspective-dependent image such as the one in Figure 1.7, the view a person takes on an object or situation or event matters to the beliefs that are formed, the inferences that are generated and the actions that

Figure 1.7 Cup or Faces Effect? Pixabay Image is licensed under CC BY-SA 3.0.

subsequently ensue. Gestalt psychologists studied people's perspectives using images that afforded a *figure-ground* perception such as the one shown in Figure 1.7 (Rock & Palmer, 1990). At any one time, the image can be perceived by focusing on the figure (two faces) or the ground (vase). If you focus on the figure, you claim the perception of two faces and can generate inferences such as what those faces are doing. If you focus on the ground, the claim is about vase and the type of vase it is.

The implementation of social and emotional programs and assessments is predicated on how we view children, ourselves as educators and the objectives of social and emotional programs and assessments. The figure-ground image shown in Figure 1.7 can serve as a demonstration. Some of us look at Figure 1.7 and think the image is obvious. Surely, it is an image of two silhouetted faces in profile staring at each other. However, the obvious image to us may, in fact, look different to others. Others might see the obvious image as the white vase in the center. One perspective – the faces – may be the standout figure to some of us while the vase rests in the background. For others, the vase is the standout figure while the faces are in the background. Similarly, the implementation of social and emotional programming and assessment is dependent on what we see as the standout objective. A dominant perspective on social and emotional programming and assessment is the perspective of adults – the school administrators, teachers and even what the parents wish to realize in children's achievement and behaviors. This perspective may focus more on what benefits adults than what children may wish to see such as teaching children how to follow rules, listen to adults and avoid conflict. In this perspective, decisions about what to teach children and how to assess them are often made without consulting children directly. Children's human rights are often left in the background. It is simply assumed that children will benefit from what expert adults decide is in the best interest of children. Within this perspective, it is also understood that teachers will properly implement the program and assessment as part of their professional code of conduct. However, this perspective is not only naïve but also exclusionary. This adult perspective fails to explicitly consider children's unique voices, circumstances and culture. A child's perspective on social and emotional programming may be different from an adult's perspective. For example, a young girl may wish to learn to become more assertive or even competitive in her studies; a young boy may wish to be allowed to engage in more solitary study. However, the perspectives that originate from children are often left in the background much like the vase in Figure 1.7 because the dominant adult perspective focuses on the two faces.

Children's interests cannot be understood or even decided simply by surveying adults. The professional code of conduct exercised by teachers cannot be assumed to serve children's best interests if children are not consulted. Rather, any type of social and emotional programming and assessment initiative from a children's rights perspective must consider children's human rights in *detailed* form. This includes *specific provisions* to survey children about what they think and how to include their perspectives in decisions to be followed in the classroom (see

Figure 1.6). In this perspective, moreover, the observance of children's rights is not only a matter of professional conduct but rather a lawful matter that pertains to teachers as *duty bearers* and children as *rights holders*. When children are perceived to be lawful rights holders in the classroom, then a teacher's pedagogical decisions are not simply academic or professional matters to be decided independently by a teacher's consultation with colleagues, administrators and parents. Rather, now, the pedagogical decisions, including relationships teachers share with students, must be viewed as needing the input of children directly. This requires viewing children as a critical stakeholder group in their own education.

Summary of Five Key Points

In this chapter, five key points were made. These include the following:

- Three basic principles underwrite human learning – these are summarized as follows: (1) *There is little cognitive learning for children without social and emotional readiness and wellbeing.* (2) *Social and emotional readiness and wellbeing can be formally or informally measured to yield data and inform interpretations about what is in the best interest of students.* (3) *Facilitating children's acquisition of social and emotional competencies, attributes and/or skills in the classroom requires earning children's trust.*
- Social and emotional readiness and wellbeing consists of two inter-related processes. The first process is social and involves being part of a group of learners that collaborates for the purpose of achieving learning goals. This process requires students to acquire ways of behaving that allow them to advance their own learning without hindering the learning of others. The second process is emotional and involves developing a sense of awareness about how to use affect – both negative and positive – constructively to achieve desired learning goals. The operationalization of

these processes depends on the specific situation and students of interest.

- Children's ability to trust is contingent on the healthiness of *attachment* as determined by a child's biological characteristics and the nature of the environment in which the child lives. A child's secondary attachment to a teacher affects the social and emotional readiness and wellness of the child in the learning environment. Children's secure attachment to teachers is called a *pedagogical alliance.*

- The assessment of social and emotional competencies, of which a child's readiness to learn and wellbeing are a core part, will often involve using a variety of measurement tools and techniques (McKown, 2019). In fact, an explicit recognition that there is no *one size fits all* is part of the mindset that teachers need to acquire and bring to the learning environment.

- The perspective of the *child as a developing person* who necessitates protection, provision and promotion as per the CRC can serve to safeguard children as rights holders in social and emotional learning and assessment initiatives. This perspective is necessary to balance the codified viewpoints that originate from professional teaching organizations but include little about the explicit protection, provision and promotion of children, including what they think about what is happening and being done to them in classrooms.

Notes

1 Attributes, competencies and skills are used interchangeably in this book.

2 Anger or other negative emotions can in some cases lead to positive outcomes. This is especially true when the emotion is recognized and channeled to drive a productive solution to a problem. For example, a girl who feels angry because she perceives a teacher engaging in discriminatory behavior may channel this emotion to increase her performance efforts and/or change the classroom climate by invoking a discussion with the teacher about the differences between the genders (see Leighton, 2022).

References

Ainsworth, M.D., & Bell, S.M. (1970). Attachment, exploration, and separation: Illustrated by the behavior of one-year-olds in a strange situation. *Child Development*, *41*(1), 49–67. https://doi.org/10.2307/1127388

Alberta Teachers Association. (2021a). *Code of professional conduct.* https://www.teachers.ab.ca/TheTeachingProfession/Professional-Conduct/Pages/CodeofProfessionalConduct.aspx

Alberta Teachers Association. (2021b). *Teachers rights and responsibilities.* https://www.teachers.ab.ca/TheTeachingProfession/Teachers%20Rights%20and%20Responsibilities/Pages/Teachers%20Rights%20and%20Responsibilities.aspx

Aldrup, K., Klusmann, U., & Lüdtke, O. (2020). Reciprocal associations between students' mathematics anxiety and achievement: Can teacher sensitivity make a difference? *Journal of Educational Psychology*, *112*(4), 735–750. https://doi.org/10.1037/edu0000398

Allen, J.P., Pianta, R.C., Gregory, A., Mikami, A.Y., & Lun, J. (2011). An interaction-based approach to enhancing secondary school instruction and student achievement. *Science*, *333*(6045), 1034–1037. https://doi.org/10.1126/science.1207998

Assessment Work Group. (2019). *Student social and emotional competence assessment: The current state of the field and a vision for its future.* Chicago, IL: Collaborative for Academic, Social, and Emotional Learning.

Benoit, D. (2004). Infant-parent attachment: Definition, types, antecedents, measurement and outcome. *Paediatrics & Child Health*, *9*(8), 541–545. https://doi.org/10.1093/pch/9.8.541

Bretherton, I. (1992). The origins of attachment theory: John Bowlby and Mary Ainsworth. *Developmental Psychology*, *28*, 759–775.

Bronfenbrenner, U., & Ceci, S.J. (1994). Nature-nuture reconceptualized in developmental perspective: A bioecological model. *Psychological Review*, *101*(4), 568–586. https://doi.org/10.1037/0033-295X.101.4.568

Brown, R., & Ward, H. (February, 2013). *Decision-making within a child's timeframe.* Childhood Wellbeing Research Centre Report. London: Department for Education.

Calkins, S.D. (2007). The emergence of self-regulation: Biological and behavioral control mechanisms supporting toddler competencies. In C.A. Brownell & C. B. Kopp (Eds.), *Socioemotional development in the toddler years: Transitions and transformations* (pp. 261–284). New York: The Guilford Press.

CASEL. (2013). *CASEL Guide: Effective social and emotional learning programs: Preschool and elementary school editions.* Author.

Cassidy, J., Jones, J.D., & Shaver, P.R. (2013). Contributions of attachment theory and research: A framework for future research, translation, and policy. *Development and Psychopathology, 25* (4 Pt 2), 1415–1434. https://doi.org/10.1017/S0954579413000692

David, P. (2002). Implementing the rights of the child: Six reasons why the human rights of children remain a constant challenge. *International Review of Education, 48*, 259–263. https://doi.org/10.1023/A:1020361511359

Denham, S.A., Bassett, H.H., Mincic, M., Kalb, S., Way, E., Wyatt, T., & Segal, Y. (2012). Social-emotional learning profiles of preschoolers' early school success: A person-centered approach. *Learning and Individual Differences, 22*(2), 178–189. https://doi.org/10.1016/j.lindif.2011.05.001

Directions Evidence and Policy Research Group. (June 17, 2016). *Racism in schools: A barrier to education among Aboriginal students. Submitted to BC Ministry of Education.* Retrieved on March 1 from https://www2.gov.bc.ca/assets/gov/education/ways-to-learn/aboriginal-education/abed-antiracism-research.pdf

Durlak, J.A., Weissberg, R.P., Dymnicki, A.B., Taylor, R.D., & Schellinger, K.B. (2011). The impact of enhancing students' social and emotional learning: A meta-analysis of school-based universal interventions. *Child Development, 82*, 405–432.

Duschinsky, R. (2020). *Cornerstones of attachment research.* New York City: Oxford University Press.

Dweck, C.S. (2017). From needs to goals and representations: Foundations for a unified theory of motivation, personality, and development. *Psychological Review, 124*, 689–719. https://doi.org/10.1037/rev0000082

Dweck, C.S., & Yeager, D.S. (2019). Mindsets: A view from two eras. *Perspectives on Psychological Science, 14*(3), 481–496. https://doi.org/10.1177/1745691618804166

Forster, M., Gower, A.L., Borowsky, I.W., & McMorris, B.J. (2017). Associations between adverse childhood experiences, student-teacher relationships, and non-medical use of prescription medications among adolescents. *Addictive Behaviors, 68*, 30–34. https://doi.org/10.1016/j.addbeh.2017.01.004

Goldberg, S. (2000). *Attachment and development.* New York City: Oxford University Press.

Green, J., & Goldwyn, R. (2002). Annotation: Attachment disorganisation and psychopathology: New findings in attachment research and their potential implications for developmental psychopathology in childhood. *Journal of Child Psychology and Psychiatry and Allied Disciplines*, 43(7), 835–846.

Hafen, C.A., Allen, J.P., Mikami, A.Y., Gregory, A., Hamre, B., & Pianta, R.C. (2012). The pivotal role of adolescent autonomy in secondary school classrooms. *Journal of Youth and Adolescence*, 41, 245–255. https://doi.org/10.1007/s10964-011-9739-2

Hamwey, M., Allen, L., Hay, M., & Varpio, L. (2019). Bronfenbrenner's bioecological model of human development: Applications for health professions education. *Academic Medicine: Journal of the Association of American Medical Colleges*, 94(10), 1621. https://doi.org/10.1097/ACM.0000000000002822

Hecht, M.L., & Shin, Y. (2015). Culture and social and emotional competencies. In J.A. Durlak, C.E. Domitrovich, R.P. Weissberg, & T.P. Gullotta (Eds.), *Handbook of social and emotional learning: Research and practice* (pp. 50–64). New York: The Guilford Press.

Hoffman, D. M. (2009). Reflecting on social emotional learning: A critical perspective on trends in the United States. *Review of Educational Research*, 79(2), 533–556. https://doi.org/10.3102/0034654308325184

Holly, L.E., Little, M., Pina, A.A., & Caterino, L.C. (2015). Assessment of anxiety symptoms in school children: A cross-sex and ethnic examination. *Journal of Abnormal Child Psychology*, 43(2), 297–309. https://doi.org/10.1007/s10802-014-9907-4

Howe, D. (2005). *Child abuse and neglect: Attachment, development and intervention.* London: Palgrave/MacMillan.

Kim, J. (2021). The quality of social relationships in schools and adult health: Differential effects of student–student versus student–teacher relationships. *School Psychology*, 36(1), 6–16. https://doi.org/10.1037/spq0000373

Kimonis, E.R., & Frick, P.J. (2016). Externalizing disorders of childhood and adolescence. In J.E. Maddux & B.A. Winstead (Eds.), *Psychopathology: Foundations for a contemporary understanding* (pp. 365–389). Oxfordshire: Routledge/Taylor & Francis Group.

Leighton, J.P. (2019). Cognitive diagnosis is not enough: The challenge of measuring learning with classroom assessments. In S.M. Brookhart & J.H. McMillan (Eds.), *Classroom assessment and educational measurement* (pp. 27–45). NCME Book Series. Oxfordshire: Routledge.

Leighton, J.P. (2022). Affective phenomena in learning: The good, the bad and the ugly. In M.C Shanahan, B. Kim, K. Koh, A.P. Preciado-Babb, & M.A. Takeuchi (Eds.), *The learning sciences in conversation: Theories, methodologies, and boundary spaces* (SECTION 3: Cognition). Oxfordshire: Routledge.

Leighton, J.P., Guo, Q., Chu, M.W., & Tang, W. (2018). A pedagogical alliance for academic achievement: Socio-emotional effects on assessment outcomes. *Educational Assessment*, *23*(1), 1–23.

Leighton, J.P., Guo, Q., & Tang, W. (2021). Measuring pre-service teachers' attitudes towards mistakes in learning environments. *Learning Environments Research*. https://doi.org/10.1007/s10984-021-09362-1

Leighton, J.P., Seitz, P., Chu, M.W., & Gomez Bustos, M.C. (2016). Operationalizing the role of trust for student wellbeing, learning and achievement. *International Journal of Wellbeing*, *6*(2), 57–79.

McKown, C. (2015). Challenges and opportunities in the direct assessment of children's social and emotional comprehension. In J.A. Durlak, C.E. Domitrovich, R.P. Weissberg, & T.P. Gullotta (Eds.), *Handbook of social and emotional learning: Research and practice* (pp. 320–335). New York: The Guilford Press.

McKown, C. (2019). *Assessing students' social and emotional learning: A guide to meaningful measurement*. New York City: W.W. Norton & Company.

Muris, P., Meesters, C., & van den Berg, S. (2003). Internalizing and externalizing problems as correlates of self-reported attachment style and perceived parental rearing in normal adolescents. *Journal of Child and Family Studies*, *12*(2), 171–183. https://doi.org/10.1023/A:1022858715598

Pianta, R.C. (1992a). Conceptual and methodological issues in research on relationships between children and nonparental adults. *New Directions for Child and Adolescent Development*, 121–129. https://doi.org/10.1002/cd.23219925709

Pianta, R.C. (Ed.). (1992b). New directions for child development, No. 57. Beyond the parent: The role of other adults in children's lives. Jossey-Bass.

Pianta, R.C. (2016). Teacher–student interactions: Measurement, impacts, improvement, and policy. *Policy Insights from the Behavioral and Brain Sciences*, *3*(1), 98–105. https://doi.org/10.1177/2372732215622457

Pianta, R.C., Belsky, J., Vandergrift, N., Houts, R., & Morrison, F.J. (2008). Classroom effects on children's achievement trajectories in elementary school. *American Educational Research Journal*, 45(2), 365–397. https://doi.org/10.3102/0002831207308230

Preckel, F., Baudson, T.G., Krolak-Schwerdt, S., & Glock, S. (2015). Gifted and maladjusted? Implicit attitudes and automatic associations related to gifted children. *American Educational Research Journal*, 52(6), 1160–1184. https://doi.org/10.3102/0002831215596413

Reynolds, C.R., & Kamphaus, R.W. (2015). *Behaviour assessment system for children – Third Edition Manual*. Circle Pines, MN: American Guidance Service.

Rock, I., & Palmer, S. (1990). The legacy of Gestalt psychology. *Scientific American*, 263(6), 84–90. https://doi.org/10.1038/scientificamerican1290-84

Roelofs, J., Meesters, C., Ter Huurne, M., Bamelis, L., & Muris, P. (2006). On the links between attachment style, parental rearing behaviors, and internalizing and externalizing problems in nonclinical children. *Journal of Child and Family Studies*, 15, 331–344. https://doi.org/10.1007/s10826-006-9025-1

Rogers, C.R. (1969). *Freedom to learn: A view of what education might become*. Columbus, OH: Charles E. Merrill Publishing Company.

Spence, S.H. (1997). Structure of anxiety symptoms among children: A confirmatory factor-analytic study. *Journal of Abnormal Psychology*, 106(2), 280–297.

Spence, S.H. (1998). A measure of anxiety symptoms among children. *Behaviour Research and Therapy*, 36(5), 545–566.

Spence, S.H., Barrett, P.M., & Turner, C.M. (2003). Psychometric properties of the Spence Children's Anxiety Scale with young adolescents. *Journal of Anxiety Disorders*, 17(6), 605–625.

Spruit, A., Goos, L., Weenink, N., Rodenburg, R., Niemeyer, H., Stams, G.J., & Colonnesi, C. (2020). The relation between attachment and depression in children and adolescents: A multilevel meta-analysis. *Clinical Child and Family Psychology Review*, 23(1), 54–69. https://doi.org/10.1007/s10567-019-00299-9

Sroufe, L.A. (2021). Then and now: The legacy and future of attachment research, *Attachment & Human Development*. https://doi.org/10.1080/14616734.2021.1918450

UN General Assembly (November 20, 1989). Convention on the rights of the child, United Nations, Treaty Series, vol. 1577, p. 3. Retrieved May 25, 2021 at www.refworld.org/docid/3ae6b38f0.html.

Van IJzendoorn, M.H., Schuengel, C., & Bakermans-Kranenburg, M.J. (1999). Disorganized attachment in early childhood: Meta-analysis of precursors, concomitants, and sequelae. *Development and Psychopathology, 11,* 225–249. https://doi.org/10.1017/s0954579499002035.

Weissberg, R.P., Durlak, J.A., Domitrovich, C.E., & Gullotta, T.P. (2015). Social and emotional learning: Past, present and future. In J.A. Durlak, C.E. Domitrovich, R.P. Weissberg, & T.P. Gullotta (Eds.), *Handbook of social and emotional learning: Research and practice* (pp. 3–19). New York City: The Guilford Press.

2

Trust and Its Effect on Children's Social and Emotional Wellness

The first chapter introduced three principles and laid out an argument for the principles. The three principles included:

PRINCIPLE 1. There is little cognitive learning for children without social and emotional readiness and wellbeing. Some children need help acquiring the social and emotional competencies, attributes, and/or skills that will help them achieve a state of social and emotional readiness and wellbeing for learning.

PRINCIPLE 2. Social and emotional readiness and wellbeing can be formally or informally measured to yield data and inform interpretations about what is in the best interest of students. Students are rights holders in their own learning. These data can be used to facilitate children's acquisition of social and emotional competencies, attributes and/or skills in classrooms.

PRINCIPLE 3. Facilitating children's acquisition of social and emotional competencies, attributes and/or skills in the classroom requires earning children's trust. Trust comes about when teachers

DOI: 10.4324/9781003152781-2

recognize and nurture their role as secondary attachment figures and
as duty bearers in the lives of children.

This second chapter focuses on the third principle and elabo-
rates on answers to the following types of questions: Why are
teachers elevated to secondary attachment figures in the lives
of the children they teach? Why are they duty bearers? Why is
trust one of the most basic social and emotional competencies
for teachers to establish with the children they teach? How can
teachers become more intentional and mindful in the creation
of a pedagogical alliance with students? Why is a pedagogical
alliance needed before any meaningful social and emotional assessment initiatives are undertaken with students? In the process of answering these questions, I begin with describing the
pedagogical alliance in the next section.

The Student-Teacher Trust and the Resulting Pedagogical Alliance

The term pedagogical alliance was coined by me and colleagues
in a 2016 paper published in the *International Journal of Wellbeing*. We outlined the pedagogical alliance as follows:

> Learning that is high-level and innovative must be grounded within
> a trusting student-teacher relationship for students to feel a sense
> of wellbeing — that is, the experience of safety, ability to take risks,
> expressing new ideas, making mistakes in the process of acquiring
> newly learned knowledge and skills, and developing the confidence
> and self-efficacy to accept feedback from teachers
> (Leighton, Seitz, Chu, & Bustos-Gomez, 2016, p. 58)

The core social and emotional competency reflected in the pedagogical alliance is trust. Although all students and teachers can
be said to be in student-teacher relationships as a function of
the interpersonal space they share in the classroom, I argue that
this relationship is not necessarily a pedagogical alliance *if* the

child does not trust the teacher. In the absence of a child's trust in the teacher, the relationship is not a real alliance as the child is unlikely to view the teacher as reliably helpful in times of need and therefore is unlikely to seek out the teacher if the child needs help. An alliance by its definition has to be cooperative.

The relatively little research on the levels of trust experienced between teachers and students (Leighton, 2020) underscores the problem and the need to highlight the significant role trust can play in children's learning and identification with the school (Adams & Forsyth, 2009; Goddard, Tschannenen-Moran, & Hoy, 2001; Gregory & Ripski, 2008; Leighton et al., 2018; Mitchell, Kensler & Tschannen-Moran, 2018). This is not surprising. In Chapter 1, the consequences of trust for children's secure attachment to significant adults such as parents were discussed. Teachers also serve as attachment figures, albeit secondary ones, given their authority and influence over children under their care (see the first chapter for a discussion on attachment). Teachers wield considerable power in overseeing children's learning and assessment.

One would assume that trust would be one of the very first variables to be investigated in children's learning experiences. Interestingly, I have personally learned that investigating children's trust is not easy to do in school settings (Leighton, 2020). Research on trust is difficult to conduct given the personalized nature of the questions asked of children about teaching professionals (e.g., My teacher is always honest with me). Consider that some teachers and administrators may be hesitant to have students report their personal impressions about how much they entrust those individuals who oversee their instruction. Teachers and administrators might fear that some reports may be negative and could bode badly for the school, and even be problematic for a teacher's professional advancement (Leighton, 2020). Consider also that some teachers may view allowing children to comment on a teacher's trustworthiness as tantamount to children providing "evaluations" of teacher performance. Given how much critique teachers in some jurisdictions endure, any data that are even remotely evaluative are likely to become a significant barrier to conducting necessary research on children's trust of teachers, and yet, without trust between students and teachers, children's social and emotional readiness and wellness is likely to suffer (Leighton, 2020).

There has been some research conducted on how *institutional trust* within a school organization positively influences teachers' work (Bryk & Schneider, 2002; DiPaola & Guy, 2009; Hoy & Tschannen-Moran, 2003). Not surprisingly, the general finding is that teachers who work in an administrative environment with high levels of trust are generally more satisfied and engaged in teaching. Research on institutional trust appears less risky to conduct as it includes mostly adult perceptions of what is happening in the school and often excludes students' perceptions of their teachers. Thus, teachers do not have to be concerned with what their students might say.

Although more research generally needs to be conducted on the *mutual* trust teachers and students feel towards each other (Leighton, 2020), I would argue that it is especially imperative to investigate how much children trust their teachers. This is not to say that teachers' trust in children is unimportant. In fact, recent qualitative research by Russell, Wentzel and Donlan (2016) suggests that teachers recognize that trust is a two-way street and that different levels of trust can be conferred to different students depending on their actions. However, it is necessary to underscore for teachers that students are the *most vulnerable party* in the student-teacher relationship. In any perceived conflict between the child and teacher, it is the child who has most to lose as he or she is the less powerful person in a relationship where the teacher is serving as assessor. A children's rights approach to assessment, then, becomes a value system for the teacher and the school to accept accountability, as holders of power, and as duty bearers, for students' social and emotional readiness and wellness for learning. In other words, a teacher's human rights approach in the power relationship with the child sends a clear message of the recognition that children are stakeholders in their education, that they have something to say and that teachers should be active listeners in facilitating the best possible environment for learning.

It is expected that teachers will be cognizant of student inconsistencies and how these irregularities might affect their rapport, level of communication and reliance on students (Russell et al., 2016). However, as the adult in the student-teacher relationship, it is necessary for teachers to recognize that student inconsistencies are tied to their developmental growth. For example, it is only starting at 7–8 years of age that children have sufficient inhibitory controls to be able to conceal lies and therefore engage in consistent telling of untruths (Evans & Lee, 2013; Evans, Xu & Lee, 2011; Talwar & Lee, 2008). In other words, children's ability to lie is tied to their brain-based executive cognitive functions and to their understanding of others' state of mind (i.e., theory of mind). Even though adolescents may be more intentionally unreliable and therefore challenging for teachers to trust as opposed to younger children, the teacher nonetheless remains the adult in the relationship. Hence, the teacher has to be the one who attends, initiates, nurtures and attempts to repair any setback in the student-teacher relationship. Unlike the child, the teacher is in a position of power to provide provision, protection and promotion of the child, and therefore, the teacher is the one who must bear the responsibility of modeling trustworthy behavior.

The reason why I focus heavily on student-teacher trust is because any classroom-based, programmatic initiative to enhance as well as assess students' social and emotional competencies will require students to trust the teacher. In fact, in the absence of trust, it is unlikely that teachers and students will actively listen to each other and change their behavior accordingly to meet any program's objectives. If there is no pedagogical alliance to incentivize student attention and interest in learning social and emotional competencies from the teacher, programs fail. In the next section, the role of trust in the pedagogical alliance is elaborated.

The Pedagogical Alliance and Students' Social and Emotional Competencies

The pedagogical alliance reflects an answer to a fundamental question for students: *Can I trust this teacher*? In answering this question, children observe whether teachers "walk the talk" and are consistent about what they say and do in the classroom. For example, when a teacher verbally claims that the classroom is a "non-bullying zone" but then stands by and allows a group of popular students to ridicule a less popular child, the teacher's behavior betrays the lack of commitment to the claim. Children attend to such irregularities and learn how to act from such observations. In this case, what children learn is that it is alright to speak and act differently because someone in power is doing so and gets away with it. Teachers, just like parents, are powerful role models.

Decades of research by Bandura and colleagues (e.g., Bandura, Ross, & Ross, 1961; Marin et al., 2020) have empirically shown the effect of "prestigious" models on observational learning. This research has taught us that when we observe relatively similar or powerful and prestigious models rewarded for behaving in certain ways or at least not be punished, people will often copy those behaviors. Parents and teachers serve as powerful and prestigious models for children precisely because they serve as primary and secondary attachment figures, respectively. Thus, consistency between words and behavior from teachers informs children whether these adult figures meet one of the most basic aspects of trustworthiness – consistency – and whether they should believe what they see. Trusting adults to be consistent in responses allows children to learn that they can reliably turn to them for help if they need help; alternatively, children learn to avoid certain adults (see Chapter 1 for discussion of secure attachment and the lowering of distress).

As outlined in Chapter 1, observing consistency in an adult's behavior allows children to predict events and learn contingencies in their environment. The ability to predict events in one's environment allows human beings to develop strategies for problem-solving to help reduce distress such as a child being able to depend on a teacher for assistance if the child is feeling under assault in the classroom. One of the elements of securely attached children is their experience of being able to reliably seek out and obtain comfort or help from key adult figures (Pianta, 2016). However, consistency or reliability is not the only element needed for trusting relationships to be formed with students. In addition to consistency, Hoy and Tschannen-Moran (2003; see also Hoy & Tschannen-Moran, 1999) identified another four facets of trusting relationships that are unique but yet interrelated and reciprocally supportive: (1) benevolence, (2) competence, (3) honesty and (4) openness. Moreover, according to Burke, Sims, Lazzara and Salas (2007), two elements of trusting relationships include an ability and willingness for individuals to be vulnerable (see also Mayer & Davis, 1999). Vulnerability allows individuals to recognize wrongdoing and engage in honest dialogue without fear of repercussions; in trusting relationships, individuals understand that mutual interests will be protected and promoted (Dirks, 2000; Mayer, Davis, & Schoorman, 1995).

These many elements of trusting relationships permit the individuals involved, especially the less powerful person, to be beneficiaries of the relationship. The primary beneficiary in student-teacher relationships is the child as the child relies on the teacher – the more powerful party – to engage in several actions in the child's best interest. For example, the teacher looks out for the new child in the classroom, assesses or evaluates the child and provides feedback to him or her for improvement in classroom learning. We often take for granted the vulnerability that is required from children to learn publicly, in front of other students, where deficiencies and comparisons are going to be made explicitly or not by the teacher or other students. This would be especially relevant in classroom learning environments where children are not only learning basic curricular knowledge and skills but also learning how to regulate themselves and work interpersonally with others. By exploring different ways of being and behaving in their social and emotional responses, children's early personal identities are taking form (Thompson, 1998).

In environments where the child is learning intra- and interpersonal skills, the child is dependent on the teacher to (a) create learning conditions that are *benevolent* in how the child is viewed and treated, (b) show *competence* in what is disseminated, (c) be *honest* about evaluations and (d) demonstrate *openness* to distinct ways of teaching so that the child has the best opportunity to learn. Of course, *consistency* in practice is also necessary for the child to learn to predict outcomes from given inputs. In other words, the child needs to experience the feeling that *in this public learning environment of the classroom, the teacher will not neglect, harm or in some other way disadvantage me.* Thus, meaningful learning, and especially social and emotional competencies, can only be enhanced when trusting student-teacher relationships exist because the child must be able to trust that his or her interests are being served.

The pedagogical alliance, when it exists, answers the fundamental question for children about whether they can trust their teacher. If yes, then children can look to their teachers for meaningful help as they attempt to learn the many knowledge, skill and social and emotional competencies that teachers and school leaders wish for children to learn. In terms of social and emotional competencies, specifically, the teacher within this pedagogical alliance also serves as a model for children. The teacher models the benefits of being truthful in one's learning approaches and dealings with other human beings. The pedagogical alliance serves as a clear opportunity for teachers to not only explicitly teach children about how to behave and treat others but also serves as an opportunity for teachers to *implicitly* model the related competencies of recognizing and learning from mistakes, apologizing, rectifying behavior and resilience.

All human beings make mistakes. Therefore, teachers will make mistakes in their handling of relationships with students. It would be unusual to expect teachers to be perfect role models in their everyday dealings with children especially given the fluidity of activities and discussions that occur in the classroom with groups of youngsters or even young adults. Spontaneity and authenticity are markers of any healthy relationship but they do come with potential for mistakes to be made. Inconsistencies in word and action will be observed on occasion even from the most well-intentioned teacher. However, uncorrected mistakes can erode trust for the child. When mistakes are made, it is imperative that teachers correct these mistakes explicitly with the child. These setbacks serve as opportunities to discuss and model for children the social and emotional competencies that can be developed with open channels of communication in the remedying of missteps. Based on the power of observational learning, three of the most useful self-regulatory *competencies* that cut across the cognitive, emotional and social spectrum for teachers to practice and model for children are *self-reflection*, *non-defensiveness* and *self-correction*. By overtly reflecting on the relationship with students, showing the benefits of minimizing defensiveness or the need to show power, and modeling self-corrective strategies, teachers can work to repair potential mistakes with students and model essential self-regulatory competencies for students. In the next section, some of the key research on student-teacher relationships is outlined to show that teachers' actions and inactions affect students' level of wellbeing and their social and emotional competencies.

Synthesizing Key Research on Student-Teacher Relationships

Luckily there is a lot of research on the effects of student-teacher relationships on student outcomes, including many meta-analyses of studies (e.g., Cornelius-White, 2007; Jennings & Greenberg, 2009; Quin, 2017; Roorda, Koomen, Spilt, & Oort, 2011; Thapa, Cohen, Guffey, & Higgins-D'Alessandro, 2013). For example, a recent review published in *Review of Educational Research* by Daniel Quin (2017) provides one of the most current compilations of the studies specifically related to the association between student-teacher relationships and students' engagement, where engagement is defined broadly to include not only aspects of academic success but also enjoyment and commitment to school. Previous reviews, such as those conducted by Cornelius-White (2007), Jennings and Greenberg (2009) and Roorda et al. (2011), have laid the integrative groundwork for some of what we know about how student-teacher relationships affect student outcomes.

The groundwork that has been done prior to the latest meta-analysis by Quin (2017) is noteworthy to cover here, if only briefly. It demonstrates what we have known about the effects of teachers on students' academic and social-emotional wellness for some time. In fact, Cornelius-White (2007, p. 134) concluded his study with a call for more advocacy and not additional research based on the findings:

> Perhaps more important than further research is advocacy for the robust associations of positive teacher-student relationships with student success, especially as concerned with the growing importance of affective or behavioral outcomes and learner-centered education's unusually high relationship with affective or behavioral outcomes (Lambert & McCombs, 1998).
>
> (Cornelius-White, 2007, p. 134)

Cornelius-White's (2007) conclusion on student outcomes emerged from his meta-analysis of studies related to the overall effect of learner-centered, student-teacher relationships. Learner-centered relationships were described as humanistic and holistic, including behavioral (e.g., participation, drop-out prevention), cognitive (e.g., critical and creative thinking, math achievement) and with emotional (e.g., satisfaction, self-efficacy) elements. Specifically, Cornelius-White (2007) found that teachers who conveyed a commitment to learner-centeredness, such as non-directivity, empathy, warmth and encouragement of higher-order thinking, showed the strongest association to positive student outcomes. Teachers who provided encouragement to learn and showed adaptation to student differences were also more likely to be related with positive student outcomes but less strongly than those teachers with an overall learner-centeredness approach. Teachers who showed genuineness and held specific learner-centered beliefs were the least related to positive student outcomes, probably because these attributes were less connected to influencing a teacher's actual behaviors. These associations between teacher attributes and student outcomes remained after controlling for teacher gender and ethnicity, and even after controlling for whose perspective was measured on the relationship (i.e., the relationship from a student's or teacher's viewpoint).

Building on Cornelius-White's work, Roorda et al. (2011) investigated the effects of positive and negative student-teacher relationships on student outcomes, with a specific focus on achievement and engagement. Roorda et al.'s meta-analysis is of special interest for two reasons. First, they investigated student-teacher relationships based on relational dimensions originating from parent-child attachment theory (Sabol & Pianta, 2011), namely, closeness (i.e., warmth and openness), conflict (i.e., inconsistent and intimidating interactions) and dependency (i.e., anxious). As I pointed out in the first chapter, attachment theory may be one of the best theoretical lenses with which to view student-teacher relationships because of the significant time and authority teachers spend and have in children's lives, respectively. Second, the evaluation of effects arising from *negative* student-teacher relationships is of considerable interest because, as Roorda et al. indicate, studies show that negative relationships can have a potentially stronger effect on students' adjustment in school than even positive relationships (DiLalla, Marcus, & Wright-Phillips, 2004, Hamre & Pianta, 2001; see also Baumeister, Bratslavsky, Finkenauer, & Vohs, 2001).

In their meta-analysis, Roorda et al. (2011) used Fredricks, Blumenfeld and Paris' (2004) organization of student engagement as one of the outcome variables, which included behavioral (i.e., participation in academics), cognitive (i.e., inclination to devote effort in learning difficult material) and emotional (i.e., positive and negative impressions of what is happening in school) aspects. Student achievement was operationalized as assessment or learning outcomes involving test scores and/or grades. The results from Roorda et al.'s meta-analysis revealed that both positive and negative student-teacher relationships were significantly linked to student engagement, as well as student achievement. However, of the two outcome variables, it was *student engagement* that was more strongly associated with student-teacher relationships than achievement. The strength of the association between student-teacher relationships and engagement is supported by the view that the way in which teachers actually help students is by working to enhance students' sense of belonging in the classroom (Hamre & Pianta, 2001); only after students feel adjusted to their environment do teachers find it possible to focus students' attention on learning.[1]

Roorda et al. also found that negative student-teacher relationships showed stronger associations to student engagement at the primary school level than positive student-teacher relationships. However, this was not found for students at the secondary school level. In other words, negative student-teacher relationships appear to be more *damaging* to younger children's engagement than to older students in junior-high and high school. Moreover, negative student-teacher relationships showed particularly strong associations for students with *learning difficulties*. This is a pertinent finding because it is precisely those students who struggle the most in the classroom that need and depend on good relations with teachers to obtain appropriate support.

At the secondary school level, positive student-teacher relationships showed stronger associations to adolescent engagement and achievement in school than negative student-teacher relationships. This may be the case for older students because, at secondary levels, there is greater autonomy and access to more teachers than for younger students who depend more on a single teacher. Thus, one teacher's lack of empathy at the secondary level might have less influence on a particular student if most other teachers in the student's life are warmer and more supportive. In addition, from a developmental perspective, older students would be exercising more academic autonomy than younger students, and so could be expected to show greater indifference or even detachment from teachers deemed to be unhelpful. However, if older students become so indifferent and/or detached that they routinely miss class or drop out of school, this is a group of students that can no longer respond to surveys about the damaging aspects of negative student-teacher relationships. Thus, one of the limitations with the conclusion that negative student-teacher relationships do not affect older students as much as younger students is that this could be due to some sampling bias. The relevant students who are most needed to report the harmful effect of negative student-teacher relationships at the secondary levels have already exercised their autonomy and left school.

Honing in on the association between student-teacher relationships and student engagement at the secondary level of schooling, Quin (2017) conducted a systematic review of cross-sectional and longitudinal studies. The review of longitudinal studies was particularly relevant as it addressed the critical question of whether student-teacher relationships could be used to predict the level of student engagement *over time*. Showing a temporally continuous relationship between these variables by means of statistical modeling can add support to claims about the influential effect of interactions between students and teachers on students' connection to school. In Quin's (2017) review, engagement was defined broadly to include students' psychological engagement, including excitement, commitment and motivation for school, academic grades, school attendance, disruptive behaviors, suspension and dropout. Overall, Quin found that most of the cross-sectional and longitudinal studies revealed significant associations between student-teacher relationships and engagement in the expected direction. That is, more positive (or better quality) relationships were associated with greater student engagement than less positive relationships. Specifically, of the 30% of studies that involved longitudinal investigations (13 longitudinal /46 studies overall), 9 of the 13 studies showed the expected temporal effects – better student-teacher relationships were associated with increasingly higher levels of student engagement *over time*. In particular, two of the studies reviewed (e.g., De Wit, Karioja, & Rye, 2010; Wang & Eccles, 2012), which included large samples and multiple data points (Grades 7, 9 and 11), revealed the buffering effect of positive student-teacher relationships for attenuating the decline of student psychological engagement, school attendance and behavioral compliance that typically occurs when students enroll in junior high and high school. Moreover, at the middle-school level, positive student-teacher relationships were found to reduce the likelihood of students' academic failure in high school (Langenkamp, 2010; Needham, Crosnoe, & Muller, 2004) and absenteeism (Veenstra, Lindenberg, Tinga, & Ormel, 2010). Quin's review also revealed that lower quality student-teacher relationships were predictive of dropping out of school (Barile et al., 2012; Kaplan, Peck, & Kaplan, 1997; Lan & Lanthier, 2003; Lee & Burkam, 2003). It is noteworthy that the systematic association Quin (2017) found between student-teacher relationships and student engagement held even after personal student characteristics such as prior academic achievement, and gender were controlled. This is pertinent because it exposes the uniqueness of the student-teacher relationship as predictive beyond the influence expected from more obvious variables such as students' prior achievement. When student-teacher relationships are shown to be predictive of student engagement *even after controlling for students' past achievement*, it supports the claim that these relationships have a real effect on students and it is not simply that students with higher grades get along better with their teachers.

The finding that student-teacher relationships are predictive of student outcomes over time provides compelling reason to ensure that social and emotional programs to improve all types of relationships occur early in children's schooling. It is at the primary levels (K-6) where most of the benefits for facilitating children's social and emotional connections with teachers and schools may be observed. Disaffected students at the primary level, who go on to become disaffected students at the secondary level may be more resistant to intervention or simply opt to withdraw from school entirely. However, before considering any intervention program, including assessments, it is necessary to explicitly recognize that student-teacher relationships are embedded within a larger system of background variables. For example, Jennings and Greenberg's (2009) review of teachers' social and emotional competence in relation to student and classroom outcomes provides an excellent discussion of some of these variables. A multitude of other variables such as teacher and student temperament and school climates are part of a larger system that either facilitates or hinders the relationship students develop with their teachers. Although the scope of the present book prohibits a full elaboration of these relevant variables, I consider them here briefly to reveal the size and intricacy of an endeavor focused on teaching and assessing students' social and emotional readiness and wellbeing.

Jennings and Greenberg's (2009) model of the prosocial classroom is shown in adapted form in Figure 2.1. This model is an especially useful organizer for illustrating where the student-teacher relationship resides vis-à-vis other background variables and/or constructs. Figure 2.1 is reproduced with some adaptations since the wording in the original model is not fully

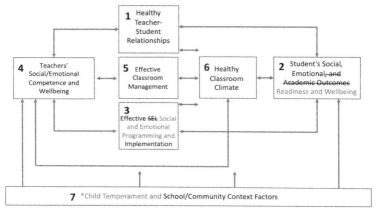

Figure 2.1 Author illustration showing first pass revision of the model by Jennings and Greenberg (2009). Their original model shows the relationships between teachers' social and emotional competence, classroom variables and student outcomes. However, strikethroughs show disagreement with the original wording in the model. Grey text show additions that reflect in the author's view better wording to align with this volume's focus on children's psychological readiness and wellness for learning.

commensurate with the emphasis of the present book. In particular, all boxes and arrows in Figure 2.1 are from the original model by Jennings and Greenberg (2009). However, text that is stricken in Figure 2.1 is done to underscore that the original wording does not provide an accurate descriptor of the constructs highlighted in the present book. For example, Effective SEL implementation shown in box "3" is better described for our purposes as *Social and Emotional Programming and Implementation* to include the selection of a particular program as a variable that can affect other variables in the model (e.g., students' social and emotional wellness) as much as the implementation of the program.

In Figure 2.1, the link that serves as the focus of this chapter is exemplified by the arrow between boxes "1" and "2" – healthy student-teacher relationships and students' social and emotional readiness and wellbeing. The main reason why I have included Jennings and Greenberg's model in this chapter is because their model highlights how this specific student-teacher link exists against other key variables and/or constructs shown in boxes "4, "5," "3" and "6", for example, teachers' specific social and emotional competence, classroom management, classroom climate and programming to assess and enhance social and emotional readiness and wellbeing. Moreover, the link between boxes "1" and "2" is also operating in light of biological variables reflected in children's temperament (e.g., easy vs difficult), and societal variables reflected in school features (e.g., urban vs rural) and community characteristics (e.g., affluent vs resource deprived).

Despite the presence of all seven boxes in Figure 2.1, we cannot lose sight of the key relationship embodied by boxes "1" and "2." A healthy and positive link between students and teachers is one of the most consequential connections to establish so as to facilitate and assess social and emotional competencies in children. This is conveyed in Principle 3 (see Chapter 1). However, this relationship does not simply happen by chance. Principle 3 indicates that there cannot be any facilitation of social and emotional competencies in children by a teacher who has *failed to develop a trusting relationship* with children.

The ability of a teacher to establish a trustworthy relationship with a child is the foundation from which teachers can build additional capital with students. However, a teacher's ability to do this will be determined by the social and emotional competence he or she has developed and brings to the profession (see box "4"). Moreover, the teacher's success at establishing trusting relationships with many of the students will be associated with other aspects of the classroom such as climate established and the classroom management observed. Thus, the assessment of students' social and emotional readiness and wellbeing, along with the interpretation of assessment results, must be considered against a backdrop of variables and/or constructs that influence everything that happens in the classroom for students. For example, children's lack of trust in teachers undermines not only a teacher's relationship with a student, but it also undermines the teacher's credibility to model social and emotional competencies for children, as well as weakens the legitimacy of children's responses on assessments of such competencies. The legitimacy of children's responses is weakened because children are less likely to respond genuinely to assessment questions if they do not trust the process. Consider that the social and emotional assessment activities or questions that children are required to perform or answer, respectively, may reveal more of what the children *think the teacher wishes to see* than what they really feel. For example, in my own research, I am routinely asked by students whether the teacher will see or find out about the answers they provide to assessments. The efficacy of social and emotional programming and claims about corresponding assessment results thus rest on the health of student-teacher relationships.

Repercussions of Positive and Negative Student-Teacher Relationships for Socio-emotional Learning and Assessment Processes

Assessment tools designed to measure children's social and emotional competencies often involve the implicit assumption that deficiencies or gains in these measured competencies are held within the child or within the implementation of a program, but not necessarily also held within *the relationship the teacher has with the child*. Although it is not shown in Figure 2.1,[2] it is implicit that a student's relationship with the teacher is not only consequential to the child's *unobserved* social and emotional competencies, but also to the measured and thus observed social and emotional competencies the child exhibits in the classroom. I propose that this is a missing link in Figure 2.1, and that it needs to be distinguished from the general construct of students' social and emotional readiness and wellbeing. Distinguishing the construct of interest – a child's social and emotional readiness and wellness – from its measurement is necessary in order to appreciate the threats to the validity of inferences made about the status of children's social and emotional competencies.

Figure 2.2 includes two additional variables and links that do not appear in Figure 2.1. First, the *assessment of* social and emotional readiness and wellbeing in children. This variable has been placed below the box showing the construct of

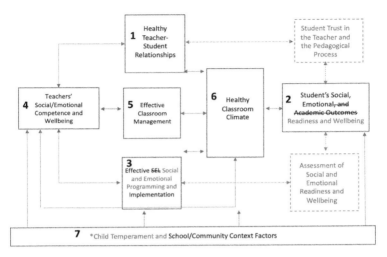

Figure 2.2 Author illustration showing further reworking of Jennings and Greenberg's (2009) model. Two variables have been added that are considered critical in the author's view: (a) student's trust in the teacher and the pedagogical process and (b) assessment of social and emotional readiness and wellbeing. Both variables are new to the model and need to be considered as potential mediators in relationships.

children's social and emotional readiness and wellbeing. The connection between the assessment variable and the construct of children's social and emotional competencies is made with a bidirectional arrow. This connection suggests that any claims about children's social and emotional readiness and wellbeing are based on some type of measurement – either formally or informally. Any measurement process can be plagued by errors, influence and/or bias. Although some error is always present in measurement, bias is surreptitious. Both, however, can undermine reliable and valid claims about children's social and emotional competence. In terms of biases, a major influence is the actual program or intervention a teacher or school adopts to facilitate children's competencies. Although the program may be first rate, previously piloted and considered to be culturally and developmentally appropriate for the children involved, the program may nonetheless be less suitable for some students and, in any case, requires fidelity of implementation. One would desire there to be a positive influence of such a program on the child's observed assessment responses. However, it is possible that the program may not be a good fit for all students, be poorly implemented or both.

Another variable is added to Figure 2.2. This one reflects the *trust* the child has in the teacher and the pedagogical process of the teacher to deliver the social and emotional programming of interest. The connection between the trust variable and the construct of children's social and emotional competencies is made with another bidirectional arrow. A child's trust in the teacher will undoubtedly influence the child's social and emotional readiness and wellbeing, which in turn can reinforce the child's trust or lack thereof in the teacher and in the pedagogical process. A child's trust in the teacher and the pedagogical process is distinguished from the general construct of a healthy student-teacher relationship in Figure 2.2. This is done to place emphasis on the *child's perspective of the relationship*, including the quality of a child's trust in the teacher. Children's perspectives on trust are rarely, if ever, included in the measurement of student-teacher relationships.

Student-teacher relationships are operationalized and measured in a variety of ways, most often by surveying the *teacher's perspective of the relationship* (Ang, Ong, & Li, 2020). For example, one of the most frequently used instruments to measure the quality of the student-teacher relationship is Pianta's (2001) *Student-Teacher Relationship Scale* (STRS). The long form of the STRS comprises 28 items, which measure aspects of closeness, conflict and unhealthy dependency in the student-teacher relationship. The short form comprises 15 items. The STRS has been validated in the United States, Greece, Netherlands, Norway, Germany, Austria, Portugal, Belgium and Italy (Ang et al., 2020). Example items from the STRS are shown as follows:

- I share an affectionate, warm relationship with this child. (Closeness)
- This child and I always seem to be struggling with each other. (Conflict)

- This child appears hurt or embarrassed when I correct him/ her. (Dependency)

Teachers respond to the items using a scale from 1 to 5, where 1=definitely does not apply, 2=not really, 3=neutral, 4=applies somewhat and 5=definitively applies. The initial validation of the instrument included factorial studies of the scale (Pianta, 2001), designed to show that teacher responses to the items clustered in theoretically expected ways; for example, all the items that were designed to measure closeness were more strongly related to each other than to items designed to measure conflict. Teacher responses to the STRS have been found to predict concurrent and future student outcomes such as academic achievement (e.g., Hamre & Pianta, 2001), behavior problems and competencies in primary-level classrooms (e.g., Pianta, 1994; Pianta, Steinberg, & Rollins, 1995) and peer relations (e.g., Birch & Ladd, 1997).

As impressive as the validation of the STRS has been, one important source of evidence that is missing is the measurement of students' direct impression of the student-teacher relationship (Hughes, Wu, Kwok, Villarreal, & Johnson, 2012; Leighton, 2020, 2022); in particular, the trust they have in their teachers. Consider that the data often used to validate teacher reports (e.g., on student academic outcomes and classroom behavior) originates from the domain in which the teacher presides – the classroom. The teacher has dominion over the assessments used to measure the child's knowledge and skill acquisition, and over the climate and governance structure created in the classroom (Leighton, 2020). Thus, it is unsurprising that teacher reports of the relationship they share with students are predictive of student outcomes as teachers measure those outcomes; in other words, teachers have an *authoritative role* in determining such outcomes. For example, a teacher who claims that he or she has a conflict-ridden relationship with student A but a close relationship with student B is also in the position to work, support and mentor student B much more than student A. Instruments such as the STRS capture this dependency well – teachers who report having better relationships with some students over others are likely to do many things that intentionally or not end up supporting some students more than others.

Because validation studies show that instruments such as the STRS, which measure teachers' reports of the relationship they have with students, are predictive of student outcomes, some might argue that measuring students' impressions of the relationship is methodologically unnecessary. In other words, why bother to measure children's perspectives because surveying the teachers has already proven effective in predicting student outcomes. However, this argument obscures an important source of validity evidence. First, children can provide an independent source of evidence about the relationship they share with teachers. Second, such evidence may reveal that children and teachers see their relationship differently. In fact, among the few studies that involve data from both students and teachers, there is evidence that students and teachers see these relationships differently. For example, Hughes et al. (2012) indicate that in studies of Kindergarten and Grade 2 students *and* their teachers, there is low correspondence in how the relationship is viewed. For older children in Grades 3 through 6, the correspondence improves but agreement remains weak. Interestingly, the low correspondence between student and teacher reports is not unique. Surveys of children and parental reports about the child-parent relationship also show a lack of correspondence (e.g., Tein, Roosa & Michaels, 1994; see Hughes et al., 2012 for additional elaboration of these discordant relationships). Remarkably, Pelegrina, Cruz Garcia-Linares and Casanova (2003) found that children's reports are *more* predictive of academically related school outcomes than parental reports. Likewise, McElhaney, Antonishak and Allen (2008) found that adolescents' direct reports of their social support systems were better predictors of improvements in psychosocial adjustments than other data. Thus, these studies suggest that it is possible that a teacher may report a close relationship with a student but the student may see the relationship differently, perhaps more distant. Another reason to gather evidence from children is to help evaluate the unique role of the teacher in delivering and administering social and emotional programs and assessments (Leighton, 2020).

The finding that students and teachers may see their relationship differently is intriguing but not surprising. Students are in vulnerable positions in the relationship they share with teachers, who serve as attachment and authority figures. As soon as children are developmentally able to figure out what they have to do to get along with teachers, they will do. Indeed, the social awareness children acquire and deploy to make sense of their school years is documented beautifully in John Holt's (1964) *How Children Fail*. Children's social cognition is well underway as soon as they enter Kindergarten, and it matures quickly as they take in their surroundings during the elementary school years. The following excerpt from Holt's (1964) first-hand account illustrates the upshot of this adeptness: "It doesn't take children long to figure out their teachers. Some of these kids already know that what pays off with us is plenty of talk, lots of ideas, even if they are wild..." (p. 40).

That students know what to say and do to get along with teachers suggests that measuring their trust and/or experiences with teachers is also potentially fraught with challenges. First, students may be hesitant to criticize teachers, even in confidential interviews, if they fear retaliation from teachers. Although I am not aware of any published studies that have specifically investigated students' hesitancy in reporting levels of trust, Hargreaves (2013) did find that some nine- and ten-year olds interviewed were reluctant in making comments about a teacher's feedback processes, as the following excerpt shows:

> **During the two terms of interviewing, the children sometimes expressed doubt about this confidentiality and were keen to be reassured that their teacher would not know what they had said...This fear was partly fear that their teacher would become angry with them about their comments, which seems counter-intuitive given the teacher's mild manner...**
>
> (Hargreaves, 2013, p. 234)

Although a child's fear of retaliation by a teacher may be unfounded, the child's fear is nonetheless rooted in the internal working model he or she has created about relationships with this attachment figure. If we accept the premise that teachers function as secondary attachment figures (see Chapter 1 for a discussion) with substantial authority in the classroom relative to children, then a child is likely to view the teacher in similar ways as the child views parental authority. Depending on the child's experiences with parenting practices and punitive discipline, the child's internal working model may well include contingencies about the negative consequences that result from speaking out against an authority figure. Thus, investigators have to be cautious about how to ask children, especially younger children, to comment about their feelings and experiences with teachers. Toward this end, psychologists who have experience with clinically interviewing children may be in better positions to ask questions than other professionals (see Ginsburg, 1997; Leighton, 2019).

The upshot of the research on student-teacher relationships, then, is that this research is complicated to conduct and interpret but necessary to recognize and use if there is genuine commitment to understanding and helping students' social and emotional readiness and wellbeing. This research is clearly necessary because teachers have an effect on students; however, it is complicated to evaluate the magnitude of these effects. Unfortunately, the methods to assess the student-teacher relationship have routinely taken a somewhat simplistic approach with the use of surveys, and without considering the perspective of the child in collecting survey data. Although the typical approach to measuring student-teacher relationships has been done with surveys, these data can be supplemented and enhanced by conducting classroom observations. For example, the *Classroom Assessment Scoring System*[TM] (CLASS[TM]; Pianta, La Paro & Hamre, 2008) is a thoroughly researched, evidence-based observational instrument developed at the School Center for Advanced Study of Teaching and Learning. (Information about the CLASS[TM] can be found at https://education.virginia.edu/classroom-assessment-scoring-system). Based on attachment theory, the CLASS[TM] was developed to measure the quality of student-teacher interactions in the classroom and the overall classroom climate.

The CLASS^{TM} is a proprietary tool. The cost is not inexpensive and would not typically be borne by a teacher but, rather, by a school system in conjunction with professionals who could undertake the training, observations and others who could assist in scoring and interpretation. As noted on the CLASS^{TM} site, the tool involves four cycles of 15-minute observations of teachers and students. The observations are conducted by a certified CLASS^{TM} observer, and the CLASS^{TM} comes in versions for application in PreK to Grade 12. The data gathered (observations) are evaluated using a manual of behaviors and responses. As an example, CLASS-S^{TM} (for Secondary Classrooms) involves three domains of observational interest – emotional support, classroom organization and instructional support. Within each of these domains, dimensions of interest are identified. For example, for the emotional support domain, the dimensions of interest include positive climate, negative climate, sensitivity and regard for the adolescent perspective. In turn, within each of these dimensions, indicators or actions are outlined, which operationalize the dimensions. For example, indicators of positive climate include: Relationships, positive affect, positive communications and respect. Figure 2.3 shows the full framework of domains, dimensions and indicators for the CLASS-S^{TM} (Allen et al., 2013).

An obvious benefit of the CLASS^{TM} is that it can be used to capture interactional data between students and teachers. These interactional data are likely to reflect many of the constructs shown in Figure 2.2. For example, a trained observer may be able to document behaviors that reveal teachers' social and emotional competence (e.g., speaking calmly to students), effective classroom management (e.g., beginning classes on time) and healthy classroom climate (e.g., addressing student-to-student conflict and being open to distinct viewpoints from students). As mentioned previously, these data can supplement survey data from teachers and students in efforts to build a portrait of what is happening in the classroom (i.e., classroom climate) and how facets of student-teacher interactions may be improved. With regard to specific social and emotional competency programming, moreover, tools like the CLASS^{TM} may be

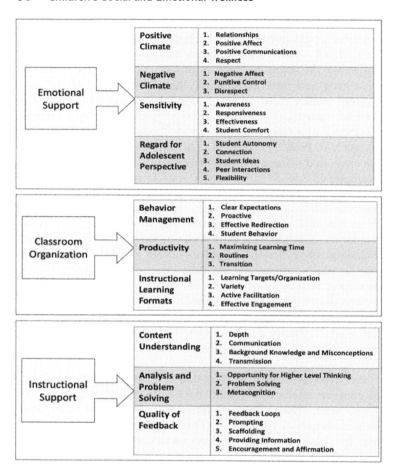

Figure 2.3 Author illustration of the domains, dimensions and indicators of the CLASS-S. Adapted from Allen et al. (2013).

helpful in the process of evaluating behavioral outcomes from implementation of initiatives.

However, notwithstanding the many benefits of the CLASS™ in its development based on attachment theory, validation across many student age groups, and as a complement to data gathered from surveys of teachers and students, there are limitations to what can be observed in classrooms. First, observations must rely on overt behavior that is unambiguously *defined and tied* to an underlying state of rapport. For example, the teacher's calm speaking voice must be tied to an explanation of what speaking calmly to students indicates about student-teacher interactions. Toward this end, the validity of any claims about the quality of student-teacher interactions requires a strong evidentiary argument linking the behavior observed to what it means, either positively or negatively, for students and teachers. This behavioral research is not robust at the present time. Second, some internal states of rapport may not lend themselves to unambiguous, observable and systematic behaviors. For example, even the most well-trained observer may be unable to detect the unique behaviors that signal a student's distrust of teachers (e.g., avoidance, lack of energy, reduced expression of ideas), or a given student's skepticism (e.g., eye-rolling, sighs, laughter, reduced attention) about the activities planned and implemented in the course of a term. Third, observations can introduce bias into the interactional behaviors under investigation. Teachers and students may behave differently when they know there is someone in the room observing and taking notes. What would probably be better than an observer is to have classrooms visually and audio recorded throughout the year so that the ubiquity of the recording reduces its novelty, is forgotten over time and teachers and students begin to behave as they normally would again. In this case, authentic interactions may be more likely to be observed.

Another aspect of the CLASS^{TM} and similar observational tools is that these tools may rely too much on behavior and fail to consider students' perspectives and voices. In the absence of actively securing reliable student reports about what they think and feel in relation to their teachers, classroom activities and even school, many investigators might miss probing the most impacted party – the student – in the student-teacher relationship. It is notable that students so rarely are offered the opportunity to speak on the record about this relationship (Leighton, 2020). Understanding the best way to facilitate social and emotional readiness and wellbeing in students and obtain their *buy-in* in response to any program, requires giving students a say in how they and their concerns are represented. Thus, while we know that there are repercussions to positive and negative student-teacher relationships as measured by survey and observational tools, we still do not know the full extent of students' experiences and how to improve the relationships they have with teachers. Nevertheless, there are explicit evidence-based guides for helping teachers begin to build a pedagogical alliance with students. In the implementation of any of these guidelines, students should be invited to comment on how they work.

Creating a Pedagogical Alliance with Students to Enhance Trust in the Process of Learning

As mentioned previously, talking to students directly about what they think and feel about teachers is not an easy task. Reassuring students that they can speak candidly about their classroom experiences is necessary but a bigger challenge is to be able to access student voices in the first place (Leighton, 2020). Teachers and school administrators may not wish to have investigators ask students questions that are personally tied to the relationship they share with teachers because some comments may not bode well for teachers (Leighton, 2020). In the process of gathering student views about teachers, the teacher's social and emotional competence is effectively being evaluated. Teachers who lack self-efficacy or feel insecure in their work environment may see this as an affront to their professional capacity and/or see it as an unnecessary source of stress (Leighton, 2020). Teachers already indicate that emotional stress and lack of good emotional regulation are top reasons for becoming dissatisfied and leaving the profession (Darling-Hammond, 2001; Montgomery & Rupp, 2005). Thus, adding what might be perceived as surplus evaluations from students is likely to be met with resistance. However, for teachers who are genuinely interested in the children they teach and want to find ways to build greater trust with them, there is literature to provide specific guidance without needing the school system or district to sanction such an initiative using trademarked assessments and programs (e.g., CLASS^{TM}).

Five years ago, colleagues and I reviewed the most pertinent educational and psychological literature for ways to define trust not only theoretically but also behaviorally, and to provide guidance on how the basic ingredient of the pedagogical alliance – trust – might be created and observed between students and teachers (Leighton et al., 2016). Table 2.1 shows the culmination of this work. The first column of Table 2.1 shows the five key facets of trust outlined by Hoy and Tschannen (1999), namely, (1) benevolence, (2) reliability, (3) competence, (4) honesty and (5) congruence. These facets are compatible with most theoretical and empirical proposals on trust (e.g., Schoorman, Mayer, & Davis, 2007).[3] The second and third columns show the positive and negative behaviors, actions and/or words, respectively, that indicate or reflect a particular facet of trust. Indicators are necessary because people do not actually observe the underlying facets of trust, for example, 'benevolence.' Instead, what they observe are the behaviors that are often categorized or believed to be indicative of the internal state of benevolence. For example, when teachers *verbalize* to students that individuals learn in different ways and *ask students* about a given type of educational material or resource, these words may be inferred to convey interest or regard about students' thoughts and feelings. However, words and actions are not usually enough to claim that a benevolent act just occurred. The emotional valence of words matters and is captured in a tone of voice or body language. A typically benevolent comment can be turned on its head if it is uttered in a sarcastic tone by a teacher. Likewise, if the teacher asks students what they think about a given issue, but the teacher becomes distracted and does not actively listen to their answers and does not come back to the issue, the act is arguably not a satisfactory demonstration of benevolence. Words and actions cannot be used as a token of genuine intention; children know the difference.

Although there are behavioral studies to support all five of these facets (e.g., Gregory & Ripsky, 2008; Jongerius et al., 2021; Leighton & Bustos-Gomez, 2018), additional research is needed to have greater certainty about which behaviors lead to enhanced trust between students and teachers. For example, Gregory and Ripsky (2008) found that secondary teachers who used a relational approach, defined as "connecting with students about their lives and being available to their emotional needs

Table 2.1 A Theoretical Framework for Beginning to Operationalize Trust and Create a Pedagogical Alliance. Reproduced with Permission from *International Journal of Wellbeing*, 6(2), 2016. Operationalizing the Role of Trust for Student Wellbeing, Learning and Achievement

The facet of Trust (Latent Variable)	*Positive Behaviors, Actions and/or Words to Implement*	*Negative Behaviors, Actions and/or Words to Avoid*
1. Benevolence – a consideration for the needs of the other person or group, and a willingness to support their interests	• Getting to know students in terms of their strengths and weaknesses by asking them questions in a mindful and nonthreatening (kind) manner such as with the following stem: *All students learn in different ways, I'm curious to know about your feelings and thoughts on something. What do you think about this material?* Example questions can include the following: • What content material they find difficult to understand or easy to understand and why; • What they find ambiguous about content material as they complete assignments or homework; • What they enjoy about school and learning and why; • How they think they can best achieve their goals and where they realized this about their learning;	• Making "know-it-all" statements suggesting you already know students' strengths and weaknesses, including how they think and feel about a topic is not recommended because it does not properly include the learner in his or her learning. The following examples provide statements that should therefore be avoided: • I know why you didn't complete the assignment/homework; you find this difficult – don't you? • Sure you know this – that's right, you always know the answers to questions (sarcasm); • You know, you really need to stop wasting time and work harder because you are going to fail this course and it may be what you deserve (verbal put down);

- How they feel about formative and summative assessments and why;
- How they feel about receiving feedback about their work;
- What time do they have to focus on learning content material outside of school;
- What activities they enjoy inside and outside of school and why.

2. Reliability – positive behaviors/words that are consistent and predictable

- Depending on the teacher to come through with what is needed or agreed upon; consistent follow-through with commitments by showing students that you remember their questions, needs for clarification and requests for assistance. Examples of demonstrating reliability include statements such as the following:
- Here is the information for the question you asked a couple of days ago. I'm sorry it took me a couple of days to get back to you;

- This is the way we always do things here – you hand in your homework and if you don't, you get a zero (no explanation; arbitrary rules);
- I am not going to listen anymore because none of what you're saying makes sense (negative responses);
- Why can't you be more like Fred (or Sally) who works hard and is a high achiever (comparisons and favoritism).

- Demonstrating inconsistency and apathy – either explicitly or implicitly – is to be avoided. The following statements are examples of potential responses that likely reflect problems prioritizing a student's needs and follow through:
- I'm sorry I'm so late with this information but I forgot you needed it... can you still use it given that it is so late?
- I forgot and I'm not prepared to answer your question (or help you learn the material);

(Continued)

Table 2.1 (continued)

The facet of Trust (Latent Variable)	Positive Behaviors, Actions and/or Words to Implement	Negative Behaviors, Actions and/or Words to Avoid
	• Let's clarify what is needed for this lesson so that we are all on the same page and there are no misinterpretations; • Please help me understand the kind of information you think would be helpful in learning this concept (skill, idea); • The test that you are about to complete reflects the concepts and skills that we have talked about and learned in class. If you don't agree, please let me know after class.	• I am disorganized with my papers. Where did I leave my responses to your questions? • I recognize that I am changing things from what is stated in the course outline (syllabus) but I think what we are doing now is more important....; • I am sorry for returning this assignment late with my feedback. I got busy with other things; • That is a great question but I can't answer it right now because we need to move on to the next assignment.
3. Competence – skills and abilities needed to accomplish a task successfully	• Having the explicit, demonstrable knowledge and skills necessary to perform the role of teacher. Furthermore, having the softer skills associated with character, integrity and authenticity that enables the effective use of domain knowledge and skills for a teacher to be effective. Example actions that indicate teachers possess competence in necessary skills include:	• Demonstrating continued ineffectiveness or lack of understanding via actions, and not addressing lack of knowledge or skill in teaching. Continued ineffectiveness sends a message to students that the teacher does not care to improve and thus may not care about their learning. Example behaviors that demonstrate ineffectiveness can include:

- Spending time during the day to find out how students learn (asking questions and observing), what difficulties they are having and designing lessons and tasks that correspond to students' styles;
- Showing understanding of the content material, attempts to make instruction interesting (experimenting with delivery) and not being afraid to acknowledge what is not known (demonstrate to students that an expert sometimes also makes learning errors);
- Showing positive and constructive attitude towards learning and in light of students' questions – uses statements such as *That is a great question...* or *That is a great answer but not for this question...*
- Knowing how to develop lesson plans and participate in professional development;

- Not knowing how to answer students' questions about content material and not following up the next day with answers (e.g., *I'm not sure why you don't understand this; and I'm not sure how to help anymore*);
- Lacking professionalism with inappropriate use of grammar, voice and treatment of students at all times in and out of school settings (e.g., using sarcasm to tease a student about being late for class but never for recess);
- Appearing confused in the middle of a lesson and then not owning up to the reason for confusion;
- Providing unclear instructions for assignments or assessments, not clarifying comprehensively when students ask questions;
- Creating assessments that students perceive as unfair and not discussing or explaining the rationale for assessment;

(Continued)

Table 2.1 (continued)

The facet of Trust (Latent Variable)	Positive Behaviors, Actions and/or Words to Implement	Negative Behaviors, Actions and/or Words to Avoid
	• Providing kind, high-quality feedback that is specific and formative in indicating what the student needs to do to achieve the next level of expertise and developing a plan with the student to help the student achieve the next level; • Providing constant opportunities for students to take part in learning and demonstrations of learning – such as *Let's try to show what we have learned in this new area...* • Managing classroom environment to be positive, respectful and constructive.	• Providing excessive information during the lesson and not demonstrating sensitivity to students' learning states.
4. Honesty – commitment to be truthful and to follow-through on promises; acknowledgment of errors and	• Showing character, integrity and authenticity, and demonstrating congruency in intentions, words and actions. Honesty also entails accepting responsibility for mistakes or events that have gone awry because of the teacher's words or actions. Examples of showing honesty include:	• Lacking congruency in intentions, words and actions indicates to students that teachers are not reliable and therefore may not be trustworthy; Unpredictability can lead to teachers being viewed as dishonest. Examples of actions to avoid include:

- demonstrating congruency between what is intended, said and done

- Admitting when a mistake has been made during a lesson or some other activity and indicating a willingness to correct it;
- Admitting when something (knowledge or skill) is not known, being willing and able to find out the answer and getting back to a student in a timely manner;
- Creating assessments that correspond to what is being taught in the classroom and not surprising students;
- Being able to laugh at oneself during moments of not knowing, making a mistake or when a student points out a mistake;
- Modeling nature of learning by thinking out loud in front of students in a clear way so that students see and hear how an expert frames knowledge and skills, and observe the recursive ways in which learning takes place;
- Explaining to students during lessons and discussion that errors and mistakes are a part of the learning process;
- Allowing students equal opportunity and time to participate in class discussions, answer questions, commenting on ideas;

- Discussing the naturalness of making errors in the learning process but then not acknowledging errors if they are committed during teaching;
- Failing to keep promises – telling a student that you will find the answer to a question raised during a lesson and then forgetting to find the answer;
- Being incongruent in intentions, words and actions – talking about the importance of fair testing and administering assessments that measure material not covered in class.

(Continued)

Table 2.1 (continued)

The facet of Trust (Latent Variable)	Positive Behaviors, Actions and/or Words to Implement	Negative Behaviors, Actions and/or Words to Avoid
	• Ensuring that promises made to students are kept – whether it is in terms of finding out information or doing something for a lesson plan.	
5. Openness – being transparent about the decisions made by being collaborative and providing timely communication	• Being willing and able to share relevant information with students so that transparency is achieved. Examples of words and actions that demonstrate openness include: • Providing a clear rationale or reason for disciplining a student so that a student understands the precise connection between behavior and consequence (e.g., *I need to ask you to move from this environment because this table is not helping you concentrate on the task*)" • Stating and explaining expectations for how to behave in class and what is to be learned in the curriculum (e.g., *today we are going to learn how to add fractions and why adding fractions seems tricky at first*);	• Avoiding opportunities to be open and lacking openness sends the message to students that something inappropriate may be occurring and that teacher may not have their best interests at heart. Examples of words and actions that indicate a lack of openness include the following: • Using unclear or vague language to communicate learning outcomes (course objectives) – saying "*today we are going to learn about fractions*" is too vague and needs to be more explicit about specific concepts and skills that will be tackled; • Administering tests and not explaining to students the objective of tests and results;

- Providing explanations when students are behaving in disappointing ways and expectations must be changed to improve performance;
- Consulting with parents, following-up and bringing them into discussions about student learning;
- Being explicit (clear) about expectations for learning outcomes and content that will be included on formal tests;
- Requesting anonymous feedback from students about classroom instruction and being open to acting on constructive ideas;
- Listening to students when they have concerns, questions and being inclusive of ideas about learning and direction of classroom instruction.
- Accepting that students may have perspectives that are distinct from the teacher's perspective.

- Being unwilling to consider alternate methods for presenting concepts (differentiated instruction) and content material, closed to feedback or student opinions without explanation.
- Using psychological control, including shaming or guilt to coerce students to think and feel in ways that are aligned with the teacher's perspectives.

(Hamre & Pianta, 2006)" (p. 339), tended to have students who showed lower levels of defiant behavior compared to teachers who conceded to not using this approach. My colleague and I also found that emphasizing the value of making mistakes in the teaching process increased students' reported trust in the instructor, wellness during the course of a lecture and a greater willingness to indicate what they had trouble understanding compared to a control group (Leighton & Bustos-Gomez, 2018). However, not all behavioral recommendations may lead to expected findings. For example, Jongerius et al. (2021) found that eye contact, specifically gaze, was associated with lower levels of patient-reported trust during consultation with physicians. Although conducted in the field of medicine and not education, the findings from Jongerius et al.'s study counter the conventional wisdom that establishing eye contact will often be interpreted as denoting interest and empathy. Jongerius et al. were also surprised by their findings and concluded: "our results challenge the current view that physician gaze is by definition beneficial to patients and their trust, encouraging continued and more in-depth research on this topic" (p. 5).

Based on our current understanding, however, the positive and negative behaviors listed in Table 2.1 are those that can be expected to lead to closer, more trustworthy student-teacher relationships. In particular, involving students' voices and perspectives in the learning and assessment process by asking them questions, actively listening, practicing cultural humility in becoming acquainted with children from diverse cultural and language backgrounds embodies intentionality to respect and show regard for students. Being open to diverse viewpoints that characterize a student's emerging identity is also critical as students become older and express their own political, religious and even social preferences. This does not mean that miscommunication and mistakes can somehow be completely avoided. However, what it does mean is that miscommunication and mistakes can be resolved more easily because the student-teacher relationship is not adversarial or even neutral, but rather cooperative as it can be considered an alliance. An alliance means that both students and teachers have rights and responsibilities, and that the teacher, as the adult in the relationship, has a unique responsibility to establish the character of the alliance. Thus, facilitating children's social and emotional readiness and wellness to learn and report on their learning requires children to experience what it means to trust the process the teacher puts in place. As the adult in the room, a teacher must oversee a competent and compassionate environment, an environment where children can be truthful in voicing their experiences without repercussion, comfortable taking intellectual and creative risks, reaching out for help and understanding that a teacher's feedback is designed to not only to serve the child's academic interests but also the child's social and emotional wellness. The teacher, in so doing, assumes the role of duty bearer and models key behaviors for the student.

Summary of Five Key Points

In this chapter five key points were made. These include the following:

- The core social and emotional competency reflected in the pedagogical alliance is trust. Although all students and teachers can be said to be in student-teacher relationships as a function of the interpersonal space they share in the classroom, I argue that this relationship is not necessarily a pedagogical alliance *if* the child does not trust the teacher.
- The teacher models the benefits of being truthful in one's learning approaches and dealings with other human beings. The pedagogical alliance serves as a clear opportunity for teachers to not only explicitly teach children about how to behave and treat others; but also serves as an opportunity for teachers to implicitly model the related competencies of recognizing and learning from mistakes, apologizing, rectifying behavior and resilience.
- There is sizable research on student-teacher relationships. The finding that student-teacher relationships are predictive of student outcomes over time provides a compelling reason to ensure that social and emotional programs to improve

all types of relationships occur early in children's schooling. It is at the primary levels (K-6) where most of the benefits for facilitating children's social and emotional connections with teachers and schools may be observed. Disaffected students at the primary level, who go on to become disaffected students at the secondary level may be more resistant to intervention or simply opt to withdraw from school entirely.

- One limitation with research on the student-teacher relationship is that these relationships are often operationalized and measured by surveying the *teacher's perspective of the relationship* (Ang, Ong, & Li, 2020) and not the child's perspective. This is a serious gap as the perspectives may not match (see Hughes et al., 2012). However, uncovering children's genuine perceptions of teachers is tricky as they may be afraid to report what they really think; clinical interviews by trained professionals may facilitate gathering of these data.
- Based on a review of the literature, Table 2.1 shows the positive and negative behaviors that can be expected to lead to closer, more trustworthy student-teacher relationships. In particular, involving students' voices and perspectives in the learning and assessment process by asking them questions, actively listening, practicing cultural humility in becoming acquainted with children from diverse cultural and language backgrounds embodies an intentionality to respect and show regard for students.

Notes

1 The mediational effect of engagement on achievement was not tested in Roorda et al. (2011) because many of the original studies included in the meta-analysis did not measure both engagement and achievement.

2 Although assessment of social and emotional competencies is mentioned in the context of studies reviewed for Jennings and Greenberg's (2009) study, it is not included in their model of the prosocial classroom as a separate variable from children's social and emotional competencies.

3 Although some investigators indicate that trust may be outlined with fewer facets or as many as ten (Bryk & Schneider, 2002;

Butler, 1991), the five identified by Hoy and Tschannen-Moran align with research on effective and congruent communication techniques conducive to building trusting bonds.

References

Adams, C., & Forsyth, P. (2009). Conceptualizing and validating a measure of student trust. In W.K. Hoy and M. DiPoala (Eds.), *Studies in school improvement* (pp. 263–277). Charlotte, NC: Information Age.

Allen, J., Gregory, A., Mikami, A., Lun, J., Hamre, B., & Pianta, R. (2013). Observations of effective teacher-student interactions in secondary school classrooms: Predicting student achievement with the classroom assessment scoring system-secondary. *School Psychology Review, 42*(1), 76–98.

Ang, R.P., Ong, S.L., & Li, X. (2020). Student version of the teacher-student relationship inventory (S-TSRI): Development, validation and invariance. *Frontiers in Psychology, 11,* 1724. https://doi.org/10.3389/fpsyg.2020.01724

Bandura, A., Ross, D., & Ross, S. A. (1961). Transmission of aggression through imitation of aggressive models. *The Journal of Abnormal and Social Psychology, 63*(3), 575–582.

Barile, J.P., Donohue, D.K., Anthony, E.R., Baker, A.M., Weaver, S.R., & Henrich, C.C. (2012). Teacher-student relationship climate and school outcomes: Implications for educational policy initiatives. *Journal of Youth and Adolescence, 41,* 256–267. https://doi.org/10.1007/s10964-011-9652-8

Baumeister, R.F., Bratslavsky, E., Finkenauer, C., & Vohs, K.D. (2001). Bad is stronger than good. *Review of General Psychology, 5,* 323–370.

Birch, S.H., & Ladd, G.W. (1997). The teacher-child relationship and children's early school adjustment. *Journal of School Psychology, 35,* 61–79.

Bryk, A., & Schneider, B. (2002). *Trust in schools: A core resource for improvement.* New York: Russell Sage Foundation.

Burke, C.S., Sims, D.E., Lazzara, E.H., & Salas, E. (2007). Trust in leadership: A multi-level review and integration. *The Leadership Quarterly, 18*(6), 606–632. https://doi.org/10.1016/j.leaqua.2007.09.006

Butler, J. (1991). Towards understanding and measuring conditions of trust: Evolution of a condition of trust inventory. *Journal of Management, 17,* 643–663.

Cornelius-White, J. (2007). Learner-centered teacher-student relationships are effective: A meta-analysis. *Review of Educational Research*, *77*, 113–143.

Darling-Hammond, L. (2001). The challenge of staffing our schools. *Educational Leadership*, *58*(8), 12–17.

De Wit, D. J., Karioja, K., & Rye, J. B. (2010). Student perceptions of diminished teacher and classmate support following the transition to high school: Are they related to declining attendance? *School Effectiveness and School Improvement*, *21*, 451–472. https://doi.org/10.1080/09243453.2010.532010

DiLalla, L.F., Marcus, J.L., & Wright-Phillips, M.V. (2004). Longitudinal effects of preschool behavioral styles on early adolescent school performance. *Journal of School Psychology*, *42*, 385–401.

DiPaola, M., & Guy, S. (2009). The impact of organizational justice on climate and trust in high schools. *Journal of School Leadership*, *19*, 382–405.

Dirks, K. (2000). *Trust in leadership and team performance: Evidence from NCAA Basketball*. Paper presented in symposium at the Academy of Management Meeting, Toronto.

Evans, A.D., & Lee, K. (2013). Emergence of lying in very young children. *Developmental Psychology*, *49*(10), 1958–1963. https://doi.org/10.1037/a0031409

Evans, A.D., Xu, F., & Lee, K. (2011). When all signs point to you: Lies told in the face of evidence. *Developmental Psychology*, *47*(1), 39–49. https://doi.org/10.1037/a0020787

Fredricks, J.A., Blumenfeld, P.C., & Paris, A. H. (2004). School engagement: Potential of the concept, state of the evidence. *Review of Educational Research*, *74*, 59–109.

Ginsburg, H.P. (1997). *Entering the child's mind: The clinical interview in psychological research and practice*. Cambridge: Cambridge University Press.

Goddard, R., Tschannen-Moran, M., & Hoy, W. (2001). A multilevel examination of the distribution and effects of teacher trust in urban elementary schools. *Elementary School Journal*, *102*(1), 3–17.

Gregory, A., & Ripski, M.B. (2008). Adolescent trust in teachers: Implications for behavior in the high school classroom. *School Psychology Review*, *37*(3), 337–353.

Hamre, B.K., & Pianta, R.C. (2001). Early teacher-child relationships and the trajectory of children's school outcomes through eighth grade. *Child Development*, *72*, 625–638.

Hargreaves, E. (2013) Inquiring into children's experiences of teacher feedback: Reconceptualising assessment for learning. *Oxford Review of Education*, *39*(2), 229–246.

Holt, J. (1964). *How children fail*. New York: Pitman Publishing Corp.

Hoy, W., & Tschannen-Moran, M. (1999). Five faces of trust: An empirical confirmation in urban elementary schools. *Journal of School Leadership*, 9(3), 184–208.

Hoy, W., & Tschannen-Moran, M. (2003). The conceptualization and measurement of faculty trust in schools. In W. Hoy & C. Miskel (Eds.), *Studies in leading and organizing schools* (pp. 181–207). Greenwich, CT: Information Age.

Hughes, J.N., Wu, J.Y., Kwok, O.M., Villarreal, V., & Johnson, A.Y. (2012). Indirect effects of child reports of teacher–student relationship on achievement. *Journal of Educational Psychology*, 104(2), 350–365. https://doi.org/10.1037/a0026339

Jennings, P.A., & Greenberg, M.T. (2009). The prosocial classroom: Teacher social and emotional competence in relation to student and classroom outcomes. *Review of Educational Research*, 79(1), 491–525. https://doi.org/10.3102/0034654308325693

Jongerius, C., Twisk, J.W.R., Romijn, J.A., Callemein, T., Goedeme, T., Smets, E., & Hillen, M. (2021). The influence of face gaze by physicians on patient trust: An observational study. *Journal of General Internal Medicine*. https://doi.org/10.1007/s11606-021-06906-2

Kaplan, D.S., Peck, M.B., & Kaplan, H. B. (1997). Decomposing the academic failure-dropout relationship: A longitudinal analysis. *Journal of Educational Research*, 90, 331–343. https://doi.org/10.1080/00220671.1997.10544591

Lambert, N.M., & McCombs, B.L. (Eds.). (1998). *How students learn: Reforming schools through learner-centered education*. Washington, DC: American Psychological Association. https://doi.org/10.1037/10258-000

Lan, W., & Lanthier, R. (2003). Changes in students' academic performance and perceptions of school and self before dropping out of schools. *Journal of Education for Students Placed at Risk*, 8, 309–332. https://doi.org/10.1207/S15327671ESPR0803_2

Langenkamp, A.G. (2010). Academic vulnerability and resilience during the transition to high school: The role of social relationships and district context. *Sociology of Education*, 83, 1–19. https://doi.org/10.1177/0038040709356563

Lee, V.E., & Burkam, D.T. (2003). Dropping out of high school: The role of school organization and structure. *American Educational Research Journal*, 40, 353–393. https://doi.org/10.3102/00028312040002353

Leighton, J.P. (2019). Students' interpretation of formative feedback: Three claims for why we know so little about something so important. *Journal of Educational Measurement (Special Issue on Classroom Assessment)*, 56, 793–814. https://doi.org/10.1111

Leighton, J.P. (2020). On barriers to accessing children's voices in school-based research. *Canadian Journal of Children's Rights*, 7(1), 164–193.

Leighton, J.P. (2022). Not all that counts is safe for counting: Barriers to collecting learning data for assessment purposes. In R. Lissitz & H. Jiao (Eds.), *Enhancing effective instruction and learning using assessment data*. pp. 187–213. Charlotte, NC: Information Age Publishing.

Leighton, J.P., & Bustos Gomez, M.C. (2018). A pedagogical alliance for trust, wellbeing and the identification of errors for learning and formative assessment. *Educational Psychology: An International Journal of Experimental Educational Psychology*, 38(3), 381–406.

Leighton, J.P., Guo, Q., Chu, M.W., & Tang, W. (2018). A pedagogical alliance for academic achievement: Socio-emotional effects on assessment outcomes. *Educational Assessment*, 23(1), 1–23.

Leighton, J.P., Seitz, P., Chu, M.W., & Gomez Bustos, M.C. (2016). Operationalizing the role of trust for student wellbeing, learning and achievement. *International Journal of Wellbeing*, 6(2), 57–79.

Marin, M.F., Bilodeau-Houle, A., Morand-Beaulieu, S., Brouillard, A., Herringa, R.J., & Milad, M.R. (2020). Vicarious conditioned fear acquisition and extinction in child–parent dyads. *Nature Scientific Reports*, 10, 17130. https://doi.org/10.1038/s41598-020-74170-1

Mayer, R., & Davis, J. (1999). The effect of the performance appraisal system on trust for management: A field quasi- experiment. *Journal of Applied Psychology*, 84, 123–136.

Mayer, R., Davis, J., & Schoorman, F. (1995). An integrative model of organizational trust. *Academy of Management Review*, 20(3), 709–734.

McElhaney, K.B., Antonishak, J., & Allen, J.P. (2008). "They like me, they like me not": Popularity and adolescents' perceptions of acceptance predicting social functioning over time. *Child development*, 79(3), 720–731. https://doi.org/10.1111/j.1467-8624.2008.01153.x

Mitchell, R.M., Kensler, L., & Tschannen-Moran, M. (2018). Student trust in teachers and student perceptions of safety: Positive predictors of student identification with school. *International Journal of Leadership in Education*, 21(2), 135–154. https://doi.org/10.1080/13603124.2016.1157211

Montgomery, C., & Rupp, A.A. (2005). A meta-analysis for exploring the diverse causes and effects of stress in teachers. *Canadian Journal of Education/Revue canadienne de léducation*, 28, 458–486.

Needham, B.L., Crosnoe, R., & Muller, C. (2004). Academic failure in secondary school: The inter-related role of health problems and educational context. *Social Problems*, 51, 569–586. https://doi.org/10.1525/sp.2004.51.4.569

Pelegrina, S., Cruz Garcia-Linares, M., & Casanova P.F. (2003). Adolescents and their parents' perceptions about parenting characteristics. Who can better predict the adolescent's academic competence? *Journal of Adolescence, 26,* 651–665.

Pianta, R.C. (1994). Patterns of relationships between children and kindergarten teachers. *Journal of School Psychology, 32*(1), 15–31. https://doi.org/10.1016/0022-4405(94)90026-4

Pianta, R.C. (2001). *Student-Teacher Relationship Scale (STRS): Professional manual.* Lutz, FL: Psychological Assessment Resources.

*Pianta, R.C. (2016). Teacher–student interactions: Measurement, impacts, improvement, and policy. *Policy Insights from the Behavioral and Brain Sciences, 3*(1), 98–105. https://doi.org/10.1177/2372732215622457

Pianta, R.C., La Paro, K.M., & Hamre, B.K. (2008). *Classroom Assessment Scoring System™: Manual K-3.* Baltimore, MD: Paul H Brookes Publishing.

Pianta, R.C., Steinberg, M.S., & Rollins, K.B. (1995). The first two years of school: Teacher-child relationships and deflections in children's classroom adjustment. *Development and Psychopathology, 7*(2), 295–312.

Quin, D. (2017). Longitudinal and contextual associations between teacher–student relationships and student engagement: A systematic review. *Review of Educational Research, 87*(2), 345–387. https://doi.org/10.3102/0034654316669434

Roorda, D.L., Koomen, H.M.Y., Spilt, J.L., & Oort, F.J. (2011). The influence of affective teacher-student relationships on students' engagement and achievement: A meta-analytic approach. *Review of Educational Research, 81,* 493–529.

Russell, S.L., Wentzel, K.R., & Donlan, A.E. (2016). Teachers' beliefs about the development of teacher–adolescent trust. *Learning Environments Research, 19*(2), 241–266. https://doi.org/10.1007/s10984-016-9207-8

Sabol, T.J., & Pianta, R.C. (2012). Recent trends in research on teacher–child relationships. *Attachment & Human Development, 14*(3), 213–231. https://doi.org/10.1080/14616734.2012.672262

Schoorman, F.D., Mayer, R.C., & Davis, J.H. (2007). An integrative model of organizational trust: Past, present and future. *Academy of Management Review, 32*(2), 344–354.

Talwar, V., & Lee, K. (2008). Social and cognitive correlates of children's lying behavior. *Child Development, 79*(4), 866–881. https://doi.org/10.1111/j.1467-8624.2008.01164.x

Tein, J.-Y., Roosa, M.W., & Michaels, M. (1994). Agreement between parent and child reports on parental behaviors. *Journal of Marriage and the Family*, 56(2), 341–355. https://doi.org/10.2307/353104

Thapa, A., Cohen, J., Guffey, S., & Higgins-D'Alessandro, A. (2013). A review of school climate research. *Review of Educational Research*, 83, 357–385.

Thompson, R.A. (1998). Early sociopersonality development. In N. Eisenberg (Ed.), *Handbook of child psychology: Vol. 3. Social, emotional, and personality development* (pp. 311–388). New York: Wiley.

Veenstra, R., Lindenberg, S., Tinga, F., & Ormel, J. (2010). Truancy in late elementary and early secondary education: The influence of social bonds and self-control-The TRAILS study. *International Journal of Behavioral Development*, 34, 302–310. https://doi.org/10.1177/0165025409347987

Wang, M.-T., & Eccles, J. S. (2012). Social support matters: Longitudinal effects of social support on three dimensions of school engagement from middle to high school. *Child Development*, 83, 877–895. https://doi.org/10.1111/j.1467-8624.2012.01745.x

3

Assessment Data from a Children's Rights Approach

The challenge with any educational program or intervention, including social and emotional initiatives, is whether its implementation will actually benefit the students it is supposed to serve. This may have less to do with the actual script-like intervention chosen than with the adult carrying out the intervention. Of course, to determine the efficacy of any one initiative, research studies and program evaluations could be undertaken to answer the question of which initiative or intervention is best. But any such study will be inevitably limited in scope. Studies are often limited in scope because they typically rely on a few outcome variables such as students' academic achievement and/or attendance, and program evaluations typically lack scientific rigor by often failing to include control groups. Furthermore, most studies designed to evaluate the efficacy of educational programs fail to consider the *effect of teachers* who must interpret and implement the program of interest and its assessments. Considering the effect of teachers is unlikely an oversight and may have more

DOI: 10.4324/9781003152781-3

Figure 3.1 Author illustration of the teacher effect. Teachers decide
    how to interpret and implement programs and assessments;
    they effectively mediate any social and emotional program
    and assessment designed to serve children's best interest.
    License owned by author.

to do with the logistical and/or political barriers to investigating
aspects of teacher effectiveness than with genuine negligence on
the part of investigators (see Conley & Glasman, 2008; Ginsberg & Lyche, 2008; Leighton, 2020). As shown in Figure 3.1,
programs and assessments do not implement themselves; they
rely on an intermediary. Adults, in this case teachers, must interpret and implement programs and assessments; they stand in
the middle of the programs, assessments and the feedback designed to help children learn. Predictably, little is known about
how programs are implemented in the classroom (Malin et al.,
2020). Malin et al. make the perennial case as follows:

> Although there is now a recognition that evidence use can and should
> be used to improve practice, there is only limited evidence on how
> this might be facilitated at the school level.... What's more, a systemic
> gap appears to exist between research and practitioners which as yet
> shows little indication of narrowing...
>
> (p. 2)

Thus, most educational programs, interventions and assessments in K-12 education are implemented on the *assumption*

that delivery will be done as intended and in the most skilled manner to serve the best interest of children. But this remains an assumption whose verification remains unknown.

This is why this chapter focuses on the reasons why it is necessary to actively include children's participation in the collection of data about what is being done to them in the classroom. Not because collecting children's data is sufficient and eliminates the need to collect data from other sources or even engage with scientific principles of study. Rather, because, it is necessary for good teaching and research practice. A fundamental premise in the United Nations Convention on the Rights of the Child (1989) is that children are a key stakeholder in what is being done to them; thus, including data on what they do, think and feel about what is happening in the classroom can inform a teacher's pedagogy and also provide evidence on the validity of inferences made about children themselves. Of course, it would be expected that children who are given an oppoortunity to voice their thoughts and perspectives will do so in an environment that encourages *free expression* of those thoughts and perspectives.

This chapter, then, focuses on the second principle of this book, namely, the collection of children's data to help us understand what matters to children in classroom experiences and how these data may be used to specifically identify what children need from teachers to help them acquire *social and emotional readiness and wellbeing.* Tackling the question of data is tricky, however, because it can be addressed uncritically by simply reverting to the status quo of typical survey methods, which can relegate children to minor roles in the provision of data. Rather, a better approach, one that I propose, is to consider the essence of what we want children to learn in the realm of social and emotional competencies, and *evaluate the alignment* between what it is we want them to learn, *what children freely express as wanting to learn* and how teachers teach and model those social and emotional competencies for children. Thus, for any social and emotional programmatic initiative, a children's rights approach explicitly outlines that children's participation starts at the very beginning of a program, not in the middle or at the end, with a voice about what is being administered to them.

The Missing Link in Children's Social and Emotional Programming and Assessment

A weakness in most efforts to judge the merit of educational programs is the relative absence of children's perspectives about what is being done to them (Malin et al., 2020). This is especially problematic when considering social and emotional programs because these are often designed to improve children's intrapersonal and interpersonal skills. Yet, by not including children in the choice and implementation of programs, the first lesson children learn is that their voices *do not matter*. Imagine the irony of the first lesson of a social and emotional program being that this is being done for your own good but you, as the recipient, have little say about what is being done to you! Surprisingly, methods to collect data about children's personal perceptions and experiences about and in social and emotional programs are rarely, if ever, included in studies of these programs. Although some exploratory studies are being conducted, which bode well for larger, more systematic research (e.g., Strahan & Poteat, 2020), the automatic inclusion of children's personal perceptions is still relatively rare. Instead, the data sources often included tend to be *indirect measures* of children's experiences, namely, their academic achievement or socially learned behavior according to the criteria of the program (Strahan & Poteat, 2020). The assumption, then, is that programs are being delivered as intended and that children appreciate, understand and value the content of the programs. However, these assumptions are problematic because multiple variables are ignored; primarily, the effect of the teacher is ignored, and the opportunity to assess buy-in from children is lost or, worse, neglected. Both of these deficiencies do not bode well in the implementation and evaluation of social and emotional programs.

It would be foolish to present the details of any social and emotional program and its assessments without considering the context in which programs and assessments are delivered by a teacher. In other words, it is relevant to consider the climate in which these programs are and will be presented to students. It is therefore necessary to recognize that before delving into social and emotional programming and assessment details, we need to propose a defensible backdrop for such activities; one that can be *expected to improve* the overall delivery of intended outcomes. Two aspects of the backdrop need to be considered: (1) the teacher effect and (2) the classroom climate.

The Teacher Effect

John Hattie, a well-known educational researcher, has brought attention to the influential role of the teacher in educational interventions. In his long-running, influential program of research, Hattie has distilled the most effective teaching practices with meta-analyses to show what works and what does not, and by how much interventions work using an index called the *effect size* (Hattie, 2003, 2009; Nye, Konstantopoulos, & Hedges, 2004). Unsurprisingly, teachers engage in many behaviors that affect student achievement, especially lower-income children. For example, a teacher's micro-teaching, clarity in speaking, expectations of students and knowledge of subject matter all have effects (Hattie, 2009). However, in a 2013 interview with then Ontario Deputy Minister of Education, George Zegarac, Hattie's body of work was succinctly summarized in a way that a simple examination of charts of effect sizes does not quite convey. In that interview, the essential element undergirding all of the effective teacher practices involved, in some way, the student-teacher relationship:

> **Hattie's findings showed that feedback is one of the most important factors in effective learning, followed by a student's expectations and the trust built by teachers with their students. Not surprisingly, it demonstrated that positive teacher-student interaction was by far the essential factor in effective teaching.**
> **(In Conversation, Spring 2013, IV, Issue 2, p. 1)**

In Chapters 1 and 2 of this volume, the student-teacher relationship was examined as being premised on children's attachment status, and how well teachers serve as secondary attachment figures in the lives of children. Notwithstanding the essentiality of the one-to-one student-teacher relationship, teachers also hold a relationship with the entire group of students they teach. The singular relationship they hold with each student and the overall collective relationship teachers hold with all students exemplify the overall climate of the classroom. This climate both reflects and, in turn, influences the manner in which teachers address students, manage and model behavior. The *teacher-class relationship* is likely to influence the way in which lessons are taught, curricula implemented, assessments administered and the expectations internalized by students. For example, teachers who are highly experienced and in control of a class are likely to feel more efficacious in delivering a new program and offer compassionate flexibility to themselves and students in the process. In contrast, teachers who are less experienced, feeling burnt out and suffering dwindling confidence in their leadership may resent having to teach a new program.

The proposition that teachers have an effect on student outcomes is unsurprising. Unless the skill level required for implementation is low, one would presume that whoever implements a program should matter to the outcome of the program. When calling a doctor or a plumber, one is not relying only on a procedure but, rather, the *implementation of a procedure by a skilled professional*. Different professionals with distinct backgrounds, profiles of training and predilections will have unique ways of translating a skill into practice. For example, one may prefer one doctor over another despite similar training because one doctor has a better bedside manner than another. This is why individuals matter in any kind of service delivery. Indeed, in Chapter 2 we covered the relevance of the student-teacher relationship precisely for this reason – people matter. Furthermore, the need for teachers to build unique pedagogical alliances with their students will vary depending on the individuals involved. Different teachers will undoubtedly have distinctive ways in which to build such alliances but, whatever the process they choose, such relationships are necessary for facilitating students' social and emotional readiness and wellbeing for learning.

However, as already mentioned, one of the notorious gaps in the literature on student-teacher relationships is the relative absence of guidance for creating a pedagogical alliance. As well, there is little direction on how to explicitly include students' voice and participation in what is happening to them in the classroom. The literature is primarily descriptive, not prescriptive. The literature only tells us that student-teacher relationships are essential but do not present a road map for how to intentionally address and build the relationship. Thus, in the previous chapter, I discussed teacher behaviors that, based on the limited research literature, could be distilled to begin to forge trusting interactions with students (see Table 2.1 in Chapter 2). However, developing trusting relationships with students cannot be done in a vacuum. It is best achieved in a *context* in which students are also learning to trust each other and have a voice in this process. In other words, classroom climate also matters. In their review of school climate research, Thapa, Cohen, Guffey and Higgins-D'Alessandro (2013) summarize the need for recognizing this background effect:

> One of the most important aspects of relationships in schools is how connected people feel to one another. From a psychological point of view, relationships refer not only to relations with others but relations with ourselves – how we feel about and take care of ourselves. Safe, caring, participatory, and responsive school climates tend to foster a greater attachment to school and provide the optimal foundation for social, emotional, and academic learning for middle school and high school students...
>
> (p. 64)

Indeed, helping students flourish in their academic, social and emotional development requires that students feel at ease with their peers and with the teacher, as well as with themselves. How students feel about themselves is associated with how *they are treated and how they can expect to be treated.* Consequently, the question that needs to be asked is *what is the best backdrop, framework or context for teachers to use in the creation of a supportive classroom climate for pedagogical alliances, and any social and emotional program and assessment considered for implementation?*

Throughout this book, I propose that a *children's rights approach* is the most defensible backdrop in which to develop pedagogical alliances and implement educational programs and assessments designed to improve children's social and emotional readiness and wellness for learning. There are three reasons for proposing this approach. First, it is the approach that is congruent with the stated outcomes of most social and emotional programs, namely, to help children acquire a respect for themselves and others. Second, it explicitly involves inclusion of student voices, freely expressed, and their participation in the interpretation and implementation of what is being *done to them* in the name of personal and academic development. On this matter, we have to imagine children as comprising a group that embodies the slogan "*Nothing about us, without us.*"[1] Teachers should help children understand their human rights, boundaries and their emerging responsibility as rights holders. Third, a children's rights approach provides an unequivocal contract for holding the teacher and the school accountable, as duty bearers, for recognizing that students have a right to experience social and emotional readiness and wellness in their learning. In other words, a children's rights approach makes clear that children are stakeholders in their education, that they have something to say and that teachers are active listeners. But this approach does challenge the status quo; gathering data from children opens the possibility that we may not agree with or even like what they have to say.

Epistemic Injustice and Children's Voice

Writing in 1973 for the *Harvard Educational Review*, Hillary Rodham Clinton was one of the first legal scholars who began to question why children's rights were not more discernibly stated and considered in the realm of education. She indicated back then:

> The thrust of most reforms, amply supported by demonstrations of children's needs has been to persuade adult society to treat children better, but *has not changed the position of children within society or made them capable of securing such treatment for themselves.* (italics added)

(p. 492)

Rodham's words encapsulate the challenge with most educational reforms and interventions – they rest on the expertise, training and goodwill of professional adults as already mentioned. However, this reliance on adults to do the right thing by children does not bestow any real voice or participation to children themselves, except perhaps passive participation. Children, therefore, do not have the opportunity to internalize the right to be heard. In a society that aims to be inclusive and conscious of bias in its treatment of children, the exclusion of children has remained largely accepted. Typical adult apprehensions to justify this exclusion are that children are "not sufficiently mature" to give reliable feedback about what is happening to them or that asking children certain questions will "upset them." I have often heard such apprehensions from too many of the teachers and administrators I have worked with over the years. For example, some teachers and administrators have indicated that surveying children about whether they trust their teachers or whether teachers provide them with feedback that helps them learn is problematic because children "may say one thing one day and another thing the next." Another apprehension is that asking children questions about how they feel at school, for example, whether they feel uneasy or their classmates call them names is too suggestive and may plant the "seed" of unease or disquiet in children. The research on the reliability of children's feedback, however, suggests a different picture (MET Report, 2012). Children do provide reliable data when questions are worded simply and they trust that they will not be punished for expressing certain ideas (Leighton, 2020, 2022). In other words, what is often assumed by adults who believe they are acting in the best interest of children by effectively excluding them from weighing in on what is happening to them within the educational sphere is unjustified.

When one consults the research literature for an explanation for the reliance on teacher reports (instead of student reports) to measure the student-teacher relationship, it is noteworthy that researchers also appear to have a bias against what children might say in student reports. Hughes, Wu, Kwok, Villarreal and Johnson (2012) indicated:

A reliance on teacher reports of TSRQ [Teacher-Student Relationship Questionnaire] in studies of elementary students might be explained by researchers' concern that students below grade 4 are not capable of providing reliable and valid information on relationship quality. Indeed, the relatively few studies utilizing both teacher and child reports of TSRQ among students in grades K-2 show low correspondence between the two informants...

(p. 351)

Hughes et al. go on to speculate that researchers are concerned about students below grade 4 not providing reliable data. However, there is no substantive empirical evidence for this concern. Logically, when one considers data from students and teacher sources, and these data show little correspondence, it does not necessarily imply one of the sources is providing unreliable or faulty data. Another, more plausible conclusion, is that the absence of concordance might suggest a measurement problem in the instruments utilized for one or both parties. Alternatively, another conclusion might be that the *sources genuinely disagree on the nature of the relationship.*

Leighton (2022) analyzed the studies showing low correspondence between students' and teachers' TSRQ reports. In that analysis, several measurement issues arise that have nothing to do with children's inability to provide reports. In fact, one of the main measurement issues is the use of *different items* to measure the student-teacher relationship among students and teachers. If different items are used, why would one not expect different responses? The low correspondence, moreover, does not suggest that teachers' data should be preferred over students' data. In fact, what these studies show is the challenge with developing adequately worded surveys for children and adults that aim to measure a specific construct – the student-teacher relationship. To remedy this situation, student surveys could be supplemented with additional data such as from one-to-one interviews with children. Leighton (2022) discusses the value of setting up interviews with children to assess how well they understand specific items and to obtain additional information on nuanced constructs such as the level of trust for the teacher.

Instruments to Measure Children's Voices: The MET Project

Notwithstanding the prejudgment shown by some researchers who might *presume* teacher reports are credible sources of data in comparison to students' reports when low correspondences are observed, there is research showing that children do, in fact, provide reliable commentary about what happens to them in the classroom. For example, the *Measures of Effective Teaching* (MET) project (metproject.org), funded by the Bill and Melinda Gates Foundation, and overseen by an esteemed advisory group of academics, teachers and education organizations from the RAND Corporation, Educational Testing Service and Harvard University among others, has shown that children do indeed provide credible data about teachers. The MET project has as its goal to promote effective teaching by means of rigorous study and evidence-based interventions. Toward this end, MET investigators have scrutinized how to bring together multiple sources of data to inform our understanding of teaching practice. One of the most valuable aspects of the MET project is the empirical demonstration that children are indeed consistent sources in what they say, and consequently, student surveys yield useful and reliable evidence about teaching practices and student learning. For example, the 2012 MET report, *Gathering Feedback for Teaching: Combining High-Quality Observations with Student Surveys and Achievement Gains*, which is focused on the technical quality of instruments, indicated that student-reported feedback about teachers boosted the reliability and information obtained about teachers' quality practices:

> Although an individual student may have a less sophisticated understanding of effective instruction than a trained observer, student feedback has two other advantages that contribute to reliability: students see the teacher all year (and, therefore, are less susceptible to lesson to lesson variation), and the measures are averaged over 20 to 75 students, rather than 1 or 2 observers. When multiple classroom observations from more than one lesson could be averaged together, these also produced higher reliability (but a single observation is unlikely to help much and could actually lower reliability).
>
> (p. 14)

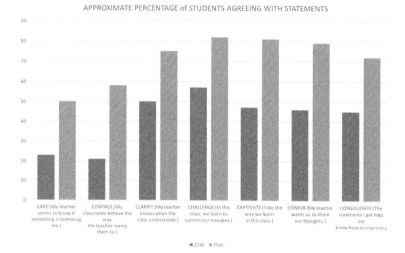

APPROXIMATE PERCENTAGE of STUDENTS AGREEING WITH STATEMENTS

Figure 3.2 Author created chart based on data from the MET 2012 Publication, Asking Students About Teaching: Student Perception Surveys and their Implementation.

In fact, as shown in Figure 3.2, student data proved useful in distinguishing teachers at the 25th percentile in effective practice from those at the 75th percentile.

The finding that students can provide useful and reliable data about teachers addresses the harmful misconception that obtaining such data from children is by necessity problematic because of their developmental status (Leighton, 2022).

High-quality survey data can be obtained by surveying children, but it does require significant attention to psychometric issues. The 2012 MET project report, *Asking Students About Teaching: Student Perception Surveys and their Implementation*, provides examples of items from the seven categories (7Cs) of interest shown in Figure 3.2. The examples are shown here to underscore the straightforwardness of the language that is required:

- CARE: My teacher seems to know if something is bothering me.
- CONTROL: My classmates behave the way the teacher wants them to.

- CLARIFY: My teacher knows when the class understands.
- CHALLENGE: In this class, we learn to correct our mistakes.
- CAPTIVATE: I like the way we learn in this class.
- CONFER: My teacher wants us to share our thoughts.
- CONSOLIDATE: The comments I get help me know how to improve.

For each item, students indicate their level of agreement using a five-point scale such as: Strongly Agree, Agree, Not Sure, Disagree, Strongly Disagree. However, in my own research with children between five and nine years of age, I used a three-point scale as shown in Figure 3.3. My team and I used a revised scale because we discovered from the clinical interviews we conducted with children that those younger than nine years old did not meaningfully distinguish between strongly agree and agree, and strongly disagree and agree.

The 2012 MET project report, *Asking Students About Teaching* goes on to outline the careful manner in which to probe students about what is taking place in the classroom, including teacher behaviors. In particular, MET project organizers indicate several areas of survey design to ensure accuracy and reliability in data obtained from students. These design recommendations can and should be applied to formal social and emotional assessment data obtained from social and emotional programming:

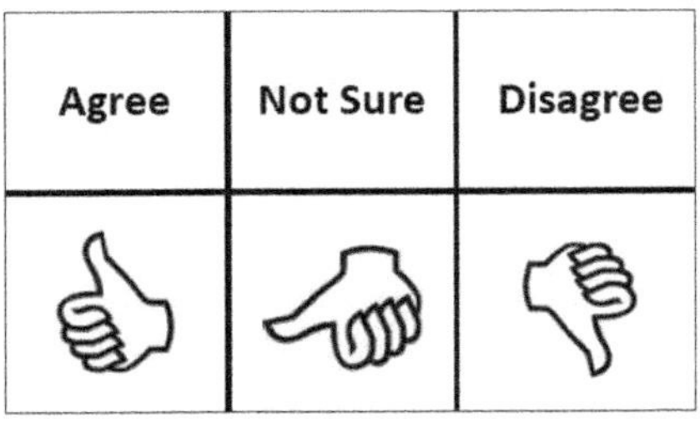

Figure 3.3 Three-point scale developed and used by Author for surveying younger children's perceptions. License owned by author.

1. Survey design must contain clear and *age-appropriate language*. Items should focus on a single idea for which students can provide their perceptions and feedback. Items should reflect classroom behaviors and events that *typically* happen in any given day and avoid having students focus on a singular occurrence. Focusing on typical events emphasizes the frame of mind students should adopt to complete the survey and minimizes the likelihood that a singular grudge against a teacher will prejudice responses.

2. Multiple items should be developed to capture a *single construct*. For example, if students' perspectives on classroom assessments are desired, then the survey should include at least five items to measure that single construct. The objective is to have a critical number of items provide a satisfactory level of internal consistency for any one idea or construct being measured in participating students. A survey that is designed to measure multiple constructs should involve subscales, and each subscale should be focused on a single construct.

3. Administration of surveys should be implemented with a view to allow students to respond freely, easily and honestly. For example, an assistant, other than the teacher, can read items to very young students or English language learners who are not yet comfortable reading on their own. Students should also be given adequate time to complete surveys and not feel rushed. Importantly, the teacher should not be administering the survey if the content of the survey pertains to the teacher. Students must be made aware throughout the administration that their comments will not be shared with the teacher, and they will not face punitive action for providing a frank assessment. Moreover, in some cases, surveys can be administered in one-to-one sessions if there is a need to elaborate on items with particular students.

In addition to these three recommendations, the revision of response scales as illustrated in Figure 3.3 provides a concrete example of making modifications to surveys based on interviews with children about the clarity of survey items intended for use. This way, administrators can verify not only if children understand the items but also whether they are even interested in responding to such questions. As an example, in one of the clinical interviews we conducted, a young girl indicated at the start of the one-to-one session that she did not wish to answer any questions on or about the surveys. Although the research I do is designed to help children, their approval beyond the consent that we obtain from parents and the school is also necessary. This is what it means to actively involve children in the process of social and emotional initiatives. Asking children whether they genuinely assent before we begin the interviews was and is an explicit manner in which to uphold children's rights to participate or, importantly, their right to freely express the wish to not participate if they so choose.

Battling Epistemic Injustice against Children

The research conducted for the MET project is not only empirically valuable as a contribution to our understanding of student learning, but it is also eye-opening in addressing the biased presumption that children are unable to provide accurate reports about what is happening in classrooms. In fact, the error of this adult presumption, which many teachers, administrators and researchers may possess, reveals the underlying prejudices that exist against so many children, and especially younger children, in the opportunity to comment on what is happening to them in their own classrooms. The lack of credibility often bestowed to children in the substance of what they have to say amounts to what Miranda Fricker (2007) calls *epistemic injustice.*

Before being referred to Fricker's work,[2] I did not know what or how to label the practice many adults have of speaking *for* children in 'their best interest,' but without knowing much about what children themselves think or would say. Epistemic injustice might be considered to be a hefty and value-laden term for simply not consulting children or, worse, discrediting what they have to say. But the term is appropriate and intentional here. Although Fricker does not refer to children specifically in her book, children comprise a key constituency in their own education. Thus, it is an injustice to not gather information from them about the activities that are happening to them. Children may not be experts in the technical aspects of curricula or assessment, but they nonetheless have opinions about what makes sense and what feels bad. Indeed, if social and emotional programs and assessments are to be administered for children's best interest, then children should be consulted as to the programs and assessments they are asked to complete. This basic first step can teach children to identify their own emotions, freely communicate preferences and advocate for themselves.

Although it is beyond the scope of the current book to delve extensively into Fricker's work, I want to outline the main idea as it pertains to children and then follow it up with the implications for social and emotional programming and assessment. First, Fricker brings awareness to the assumptions we make as individuals when we trust what others say. For example, we believe what public health officials tell us when they say that certain behaviors are detrimental to our health because we bestow upon such officials high levels of knowledge and therefore authority in their advice; that is, we recognize their expertise. However, we do something similar even when individuals do not have formally credentialed expertise, but are relaying something personal about which we assume they know. For example, when post-secondary students complete evaluations of the teaching they have experienced in a particular course, college administrators take the evaluations seriously because they assume that these personal student reports reflect truthful perceptions and preferences. In both of these examples, Fricker would say that we accept at face value, in the absence of contravening information, the truthful testimonials of the public health officials and post-secondary students' utterances. In other words, we operate from a position of believing other adults unless we have reason to disbelieve; this is a phenomenon that is broadly termed a *cooperative principle*, which has also been referenced in the linguistic and reasoning research literature (e.g., see Grice, 1975; Leighton & Sternberg, 2012).

When human beings communicate and reason about information, then, they are predisposed to believe the speaker unless there is an explicit reason to disbelieve. This is because, all else being equal,[3] we want to be obliging in our communication and, in so doing, not apply barriers to informational exchange. However, rarely does real life operate with *all else being equal*. Indeed, third variables lurk in the background and can elevate or depress a person's credibility. One such variable is the interlocutor's *identity*, and, more specifically, his or her social type or category. According to Fricker, an identity prejudice is a "label for prejudices against people *qua* social type... [namely, the] injustice that a speaker suffers in receiving deflated credibility from the hearer..." (p. 4) due to the category to which the speaker belongs. The example Fricker uses to illustrate identity prejudice is of a Black person who is not believed by a police officer simply because he is Black. The example could include any person that is associated with a category of reduced status vis-à-vis the hearer (e.g., a woman running for political office). Nonetheless, this is a particularly relevant example given what we know about how stereotypes, potential unconscious or implicit biases[4] and forms of systemic discrimination may alter the way in which others are perceived and judged.

If some individuals are presumed to have a *credibility deficit* because of their membership in what might be viewed as a low-status group, Fricker logically asserts that others may enjoy a *credibility excess* because of their membership in the opposite type of group – a high-status group. The latter, then, are more likely to be believed simply because their status confers a certain level of credibility. For example, public health authorities enjoy a credibility excess because of their status in having knowledge about the health information they dispense. Likewise, teachers enjoy a credibility excess because they spend a lot of time with the children they teach, and so are often presumed to know what children would enjoy, dislike, find difficult, or even offensive. However, in both cases, an empirical and human rights argument can be levied against harms that might result from such excesses in credibility. For example, in the case of public health officials, their advice is undoubtedly only as good as the evidentiary argument on which their advice is rooted and should be balanced against the collateral damage that the advice might have on specific groups.[5] Likewise, in the case of teachers. Teachers may claim to know what the children they teach think or how they would react to a given event but this could be wrong, especially if teachers' impressions are largely based on their own preferences or selective data (i.e., anecdote). By systematically dismissing children's meaningful participation in what happens to them in the classroom, I propose that we are committing an epistemic injustice against children. This injustice cannot be dismissed or justified by saying that children are not sufficiently mature to weigh in on what happens to them educationally. This is simply untrue. By the time children enter Kindergarten, they are able to indicate what they enjoy, find interesting and what they fear or find unpleasant. Thus, they can be queried about aspects of programs and assessments that are being implemented in their interest, and their data should be considered accordingly to help modify aspects of programs and assessments, especially those that are implemented to facilitate their social and emotional readiness and wellbeing for learning. Without recognizing and understanding that children have an explicit voice, children cannot be invited to participate meaningfully in the social and emotional lessons they are supposed to be learning. And if they cannot participate meaningfully, it is doubtful that they will internalize the essence of those social and emotional lessons.

Principles, Pedagogy and Implementation of a Children's Rights Approach to Learning and Assessment

To include children meaningfully in the social and emotional programming and assessment initiatives implemented in the classroom, an explicit human rights approach is recommended. It is my view that it is only by incorporating such an approach in social and emotional programming initiatives that epistemic injustices against children can be curtailed, and that children can learn about principles of human rights that are considered essential in most programs of social and emotional readiness and wellness. Luckily, there are roadmaps for how this can be done.

Principles of a Human Rights Approach

Drawing extensively from the research of Katherine Covell (e.g., Covell, Howe, & Blokhuis, 2018) and the children's rights education network (Friedmann & Covell, 2012; www.childrensrightseducation.com), a children's rights approach involves three basic principles, which are exemplified in various articles of the Convention of the Rights of the Child:

1. Universality – the rights outlined in the CRC apply to all children.
2. Indivisibility – no single right supersedes the others; all children's rights are equally important.
3. Interdependence – rights have to be observed as a set for children to fully benefit from them.

These three principles should serve as a guide for the social and emotional pedagogy and assessment tools that are considered in the classroom as the next section outlines.

Pedagogy

The three principles of universality, indivisibility and interdependence underwrite three pillars of pedagogy for how teachers can work to create a climate for supporting social and emotional instruction and assessment:

1. Teaching children about their human rights – children can learn to *identify* their rights by being exposed to and working with child-friendly versions of the CRC. This can be done using several examples of child-appropriate versions of the convention from UNICEF (https://www.unicef.org/sop/convention-rights-child-child-friendly-version) and Save the Children (https://resourcecentre.savethechildren.net/), in addition to the material provided by Children's Rights Education (http://childrensrightseducation.com/index.html). Numerous activities can be organized around teaching children about these rights as indicated next.

2. Discussing and *analyzing* rights – children can learn to think through the human rights they have and share with other children. They can be facilitated in thinking about what kinds of behaviors are indicative and respectful of those rights not only for themselves but also for others. Children can learn that teachers also need to observe these rights in how they deal with students. This can be done via teacher-facilitated discussion, small group sharing and child-led projects designed to prompt discussion, story-telling and questions about the rights. For example, as shown in Figure 3.4, a class poster can be designed to illustrate the contract of behaviors that teachers and students commit to in upholding children's rights:

3. Becoming intentional in *application* of rights – children can learn to think about how they are and can be responsible for upholding these rights for themselves and other children. But they can also learn to become increasingly aware and self-regulate their application of rights. Again, with facilitation from the teacher, children can be mentored in discussions about how the classroom climate can be improved to make sure the rights they have learned about and chosen to uphold are followed, and what should be done when there are breaches of the human rights to which all have agreed.

In helping children learn about their rights, teachers must be careful to not fall into the trap of censoring or shaming children's interactions, ideas and perspectives. In the process of learning how to work with each other, children will make mistakes and even on occasion offend other children unintentionally. Correcting a child's behavior should not include embarrassing the child as a person. This form of psychological control is harmful to children's learning (Soenens, Sierens, Vansteenkiste, Dochy & Goosens, 2012). To build trust in the classroom and among the children, teachers have to learn to respond appropriately to student conflict. This means treating all children with dignity and respect in the process of helping them realize that words can be hurtful but that forgiveness is important. No one is immune

Our Class Human Rights Rules

Because Every Child has a Right to Learn:
Guidelines for Classroom Behavior

 We need to start class ON TIME so we won't waste learning time!

 We need to share our thoughts on how we can get better in our learning!

 No gets left out EVER because we learn best when we learn together!

 We actively listen! Teachers and students to EACH other!

 We ADMIT our mistakes and do BETTER!

Figure 3.4 Author created exemplar poster for Human Rights Contract showing actual behaviors linked to social and emotional competencies for readiness and wellbeing. License owned by author.

to making mistakes and deserving to be heard in the process of making reparations to the relationship. Handling conflict productively in the classroom is essential because it is counter-productive to children's rights to create a classroom without conflict that is artificially premised on fear and censorship of expression.

Implementation

The three pillars of pedagogy – identification, analysis and application – must be implemented systematically to form part of the culture created in the classroom. Toward this end, Covell recommends that, ideally, the whole school should be participating in a child's rights-based approach. However, even if the whole school is not on board, teachers can actively implement this approach in their classrooms. For example, at the classroom level, many of the following practices are recommended by Covell, which I elaborate for concreteness:

1. Asking children to *identify behaviors* that are respectful of the different rights outlined in the CRC.
2. Inviting children to think about how *children's rights can be integrated into teaching materials*, assessments and overall curricula. For example, asking children to consider how children's voices might be incorporated into assessments?
3. Developing a system for ensuring that children are able to *participate meaningfully* in all aspects of classroom activities. For example, children can work in small groups to develop a working system for making sure no child is left out of giving their opinions about child-led activities, and how to kindly and respectfully deal with children who dominate discussion.
4. Incorporating *rights-based democratic teaching practices*, such as inviting students to comment on the activities planned, reflect on the assessments they complete, as well as using role-play, small group learning and project-based learning to creatively explore different ways of learning.
5. Designing and posting *a charter of classroom rights* at the beginning of the school year, alongside examples of

behaviors that reflect respectful observance of those rights. This activity can be done after teachers and students have had a chance to learn about the rights.

6. Developing a *system for continually referring to the charter* of classroom rights throughout the school term, and developing a system for resolving conflict, behavioral problems or infringements of any child's rights.

7. *Advising parents of the children's rights approach* and the rationale for the approach, including helping parents learn more about the benefits of student social and emotional readiness and wellbeing for learning within such an approach. Of note, it is helpful to alert parents of the children's rights approach early in the school year in order to give them an opportunity to comment and express any concerns.

8. Designing a student self-assessment tool for *seeking students' impressions and evaluating progress* in the implementation of the children's rights approach taken in the classroom.

9. *Meeting with students individually* and asking how the rights-based approach is working for them and how it could be improved, if at all.

10. Illustrating to students how *teachers have changed their behavior to comply with the charter* of classroom rights.

The last two recommendations are not found specifically on the Children's Right Education site but, rather, I have included them because they provide teachers with additional opportunities to create strong student-teacher relationships. First, by meeting with students individually, teachers can check in with students and discuss anything in relation to the charter that a student may not know how to raise in the context of the full classroom. Second, by illustrating to students how a teacher has changed his or her behavior to better meet the charter's objectives, the teacher shows and actively models for students that, as an adult, one is not above the charter. This is a lesson in role modeling for students; students see the influence of the charter on the teacher and the teacher's commitment to it. In the next section, I review some of the empirical literature associated with implementing a child rights approach in the classroom.

Embedding a Social and Emotional Program and Assessments within a Children's Rights Approach

The children's rights education network (Friedmann & Covell, 2012; www.childrensrightseducation.com) provides principles, pedagogy and implementation for teaching children about their rights but not necessarily about social and emotional wellness. For this reason, intentionally infusing social and emotional programming and assessment against a backdrop of children's human rights is extremely promising. Indeed, I would propose that having a children's rights approach is probably more important than any one social and emotional program and assessment initiative. I make this claim from the vast literature on therapeutic interventions, and the larger effect of the relationship shared between therapist and client on client outcomes than any one specific treatment type or variable. In particular, the American Psychological Association's (APA) Task Force on Evidence-Based Relationships and Responsiveness concluded that just as important as any one treatment or therapeutic method is the actual relationship the therapist has with the client – this is called the *therapeutic alliance*. Indeed, Norcross and Lambert (2018) in their meta-analytic review of a set of 16 studies published in a special issue of Psychotherapy conclude as one of the multiple recommendations: "*The therapy relationship accounts for client improvement (or lack of improvement) as much as, and probably more than, the particular treatment method*" (p. 308). The reason why this conclusion makes so much sense is because, as outlined at the beginning of this chapter, professional delivery matters. Therapeutic treatments do not deliver themselves – they rely on the therapist. The therapist must create a relationship where the client feels valued, heard and respected. Likewise, I would argue that the effectiveness of social and emotional programs is contingent on how students feel about what is happening to them in the classroom. In a classroom where children's rights are not recognized, discussed and/or upheld, social and emotional programming becomes a technique without any *pedagogical alliance*. In other words, the tacit part of any intervention involves how those included in the intervention think about what is happening to them, their comfort level with the process and their motivation to believe that this process of productive change is in their best interest.

As mentioned at the beginning of this chapter, programs do not deliver themselves. People deliver programs. If the person, in this case a teacher, delivering the program (or treatment) is not operating from a set of fundamentally collaborative principles, even the best program is unlikely to succeed. Thus, it is far better to work from a set of overarching principles in teaching and assessing social and emotional readiness and wellbeing than to work from any one proprietary program. Stating this may not endear me to purveyors of costly programs, but my objective is to recommend principles derived from the psychological science of student learning and wellness and not to prescribe any one program or practice.

Nonetheless, if school leadership and/or classroom teachers decide, with parental and children's input, that a specific proprietary program is desired and appropriate, then such a program should be incorporated in a learning environment that has also adopted a children's rights approach. To reiterate, the reason for this is because an integral aspect to children's social and emotional readiness and wellness is their understanding that they have basic rights and so do their classmates. There can be no substantive modeling of social and emotional wellness for children in a learning environment that lacks the openness to discuss human rights as they pertain to all children. To do this, then, I propose that social and emotional programs and assessments be adjusted to align with the tenets of the United Nations Convention on the Rights of the Child. In the next section, I talk through the basic *mind shift* that is required for this to be done. What I wish to underscore with this is that it is less about following a recipe list of boxes to check off or things to do or not do but, rather, a fundamental shift in how all children are viewed – as rights holders.

Example of Socio-emotional Program and Assessment for K-12: xSEL Labs

The most well-known social and emotional programming initiative is the Collaborative for Academic, Social and Emotional Learning or CASEL (https://casel.org/) introduced in Chapter 1.

The benefits of CASEL programming involve the breadth and growing evidentiary base for many of its programs. For example, one immediately learns upon visiting the CASEL site of the many types of programs, depending on the developmental stage of the children being considered, level of program evidence desired, program approach, implementation support offerings, areas to which SEL is promoted, school characteristics, student characteristics, evaluation outcomes and training offerings preferred. For another excellent display of options for social and emotional assessment programs, I recommend reviewing the *Tools Index* at AIR or the American Institutes for Research (see https://www.air.org/resource/social-and-emotional-learning-sel-solutions-air). What is clear from both CASEL and AIR is that the level of choice for programming and assessment is overwhelming and can be intimidating if there is no overarching approach or set of principles guiding the selection. However, a children's rights approach provides a solid guiding principle for choosing and modifying programs.

A children's rights approach affords educators, parents and children a principled lens by which to select a program that is aligned with broader values of inclusion and non-discrimination, and the characteristics of students and school. Moreover, it provides a lens for imagining what aspects of the program may need to be tweaked or adapted, based on student-based data, to be more responsive to a children's human rights approach. For example, one limitation of CASEL is that most programs are proprietary and can only be purchased at a cost. This means that economically disadvantaged classrooms, schools and families are unlikely to be able to acquire these materials. It also means that describing how to modify such programs within a human rights approach is challenging to do in a book such as this because all the materials are copyrighted. However, this should not stop schools or classrooms that cannot afford these programs from creating programs and assessing social and emotional competencies. There is a lot that can be done with open resource materials if instead of the specific programs, a principled approach is taken. Thus, in the following section, I do not focus on CASEL[6] and instead use materials from xSEL labs. xSEL lab materials are associated with CASEL but provide more accessible options. For example, the FAQs on the xSEL site indicate that "All SELweb competencies are part of CASEL's definition of SEL competencies." It is important to note, however, that although the xSEL Labs site at https://xsel-labs.com/ provides many resources free of charge, not all materials are freely available.

The xSEL Lab materials provide an excellent repository of resources to enhance children's social and emotional readiness and wellbeing from a position of *assessment first*. This is a benefit is my view because assessments provide essential baseline data for discussion and interpretation of programmatic direction and can guide what future steps should be taken to help children, with a constant view to assess progress in whatever is being implemented. Their program guide, *Data-Informed Social Emotional Learning (SEL) Instruction*, can be downloaded free of charge and provides an overall roadmap for a cycle of assessing, reflecting, planning and teaching for social and emotional readiness and wellness (https://xsel-labs.com/wp-content/uploads/2019/05/Guide-to-Data-Informed-SEL-Instruction.pdf). For example, one of the first assessments offered on the site's Resources Tab is a *re-entry survey* for parents to fill out (https://xsel-labs.com/wp-content/uploads/2020/07/Survey-Re-Entry.pdf). This re-entry survey, a portion of which is illustrated in Figure 3.5, probes parents for any concerns they might have about their child's social and emotional states. My

In an effort to support students this fall, we wish to learn about their social and emotional well-being. Social and emotional well-being refers to social, emotional, and mental health. Please take two minutes to complete this survey.

1. Do you have any concerns about your child's social and emotional well-being? ☐ Yes ☐ No

2. Would you like to speak with a member of the student services team about your child's social and emotional well-being? ☐ Yes ☐ No

3. Since the pandemic began, has anyone in your extended family experienced:
a. Illness ☐ Yes ☐ No
b. Death ☐ Yes ☐ No

c. Change in employment status ☐ Yes ☐ No

Figure 3.5 Illustration of the types of questions to include in Re-Entry Survey modeled after exemplar found at xSEL Labs (https://xsel-labs.com/resources/worksheets/).

recommendation is that this re-entry survey be used alongside a conversation with parents or guardians about the children's rights approach taken in the classroom. For example, teachers could schedule a meet-and-greet with parents and showcase the principles of universality (e.g., the rights to health, wellbeing and education outlined in the CRC), indivisibility (i.e., that no single right supersedes the others) and interdependence (i.e., rights have to be observed as a set for children to fully benefit from them), then present the re-entry survey as a way to gather preliminary data from parents, and discuss these data in view of how a children's rights approach provides principles for supporting children's social and emotional readiness and wellness for learning. The children's rights education network (Friedmann & Covell, 2012; www.childrensrightseducation.com) provides resources for discussing children's human rights free of charge.

Another data-gathering tool, which I would recommend using collaboratively with children, is called a *Defining Social and Emotional Learning Worksheet* (https://xsel-labs.com/resources/defining-sel-worksheet/). To get the worksheet from the xSEL site, one needs to register name and school. However, aside from providing this information, I did not encounter any requests for payment. I have modified the worksheet shown in Figure 3.6 to emphasize the term social and emotional readiness and wellbeing, as well as including prompts for why these states are valued.

Notice that no definition of social and emotional readiness and wellbeing is given on this worksheet. Instead, the worksheet is completed collaboratively and provides an opportunity to engage children's views in discussing what terms mean for them and why they might be important in the learning process. Thus, definitions of social and emotional readiness and wellbeing are not imposed *by others* from a specific cultural or institutional perspective but, rather, constructed by the teacher alongside the participating children. Parents can also be included but, importantly, children need to be involved at a grass-roots level in helping to define what it is they are going to be learning collectively, and on what aspects of this learning they will be assessed. For example, 'empathy' or being kind to one another might be identified as a competency or skill for social and emotional readiness and wellbeing in the classroom. Then, asking children to

Defining Social and Emotional Readiness and Wellbeing	

We define social and emotional **readiness** as:

We define social and emotional **wellness** as:

Specific social and emotional **competencies/skills** that are included:

We **value** social and emotional **readiness** because_____.

We **value** social and emotional **wellbeing** because _____.

What specific competency do we want to learn?	Why is it **important to us?**	What behavior shows us this?	How can it be assessed?	How do **we resolve** setbacks?
1.				
2.				
3.				
4.				

Figure 3.6 Author generated illustration of Definition Worksheet modeled after xSEL Lab's worksheet (https://xsel-labs.com/resources/worksheets/). Icon on the right-hand corner is the symbol for the author's Learning Errors and Formative Feedback (LEAFF) model.

think about why it might be important for individuals to show empathy or kindness in a learning environment can ensue, followed by the types of behaviors that demonstrate kindness towards others. The worksheet also shows a place for discussing how such a competency might be assessed in the classroom and what to do if setbacks are encountered. Using the worksheet as a collaborative process of data-gathering serves the pedagogy recommended within a children's rights approach, namely:

1. Identifying *what is social and emotional competence* (wellness/readiness) collaboratively with children under the banner of human rights and why this competence is valued;
2. Analyzing with children *what kinds of behaviors lead to social and emotional wellness/readiness* and how such behaviours can be designed to be respectful of all children;
3. Applying strategies for holding *the classroom accountable or responsible for observing these behaviors* as ways in which children can work together to advocate human rights for each other.

After identifying the social and emotional competencies of interest, how does one go about teaching whatever competencies have been identified? This is where the teacher can help create activities to foster comfort and practice with the competencies that have been identified as important, and the behaviors that are identified as reflecting these competencies. Toward this end, the teacher serves as a role model and coach, showing and approximating for the children what empathy looks like. This is where proprietary programs can offer ideas in terms of activities. However, we also recognize that ideas for teaching and modeling empathy and other social and emotional competencies can be obtained in a variety of ways. For example, there are an overwhelming number of websites that offer creative activities. However, the essential idea is to not become wed or rigid in the implementation of any one activity. The principle is to constantly evaluate how well implementation is working with the children involved. When ideas are put into action, evaluate how they are working, ask children what they think and collect data. Then practice reflecting about the data, and consider what comes next. There is no right or wrong here. It is a cycle of compassionate inquiry where you and the students are investigators. In the next chapter, I delve into how to reframe assessments for social and emotional readiness and wellbeing, with an eye for reflecting on data and acting on the data in ways that aim to uphold children's rights.

Summary of Five Key Points

In this chapter, five key points were made. These include the following:

- A fundamental premise in the United Nations Convention on the Rights of the Child (1989) is that children are a key stakeholder in what is being done to them; thus, including data on what they do, think and feel about what is happening in the classroom can inform a teacher's pedagogy and also provide evidence on the validity of inferences made about children themselves.

- A weakness in most efforts to judge the merit of educational programs is the relative absence of children's perspectives about what is being done to them (Malin et al., 2020). This is especially problematic when considering social and emotional programs because these are often designed to improve children's intrapersonal and interpersonal skills. Yet, by not including children in the choice and implementation of programs, the first lesson children learn is that their voices do not matter.

- Leighton (2022) analyzed the studies showing low correspondence between students' and teachers' TSRQ reports. In that analysis, several measurement issues arise that have nothing to do with children's inability to provide reports. In fact, one of the main measurement issues is the use of different items to measure the student-teacher relationship among students and teachers.

- One of the most valuable aspects of the MET project is the empirical demonstration that children are indeed consistent sources in what they say, and consequently, student surveys yield useful and reliable evidence about teaching practices and student learning.

- A children's rights approach affords educators, parents and children a principled lens by which to select a program that is aligned with broader values of inclusion and non-discrimination, and the characteristics of students and school. Moreover, it provides a lens for imagining what aspects of the program may need to be tweaked or adapted, based on student-based data, to be more responsive to a children's human rights approach.

Notes

1 The origins of the slogan 'Nothing about us without us' are difficult to pin down but it has been used by various political groups to indicate the necessity of including groups members into any decision process that will ultimately affect those members. In 1998, James Charlton used this slogan as the title of a book about disability rights. In this book, Charlton writes on page 3 that he "first

heard the expression 'Nothing About us Without Us' in South Africa in 1993." The slogan has been used by many groups often marginalized from the political decision-making process.

2 I wish to thank a fellow participant from the 2021 Leiden University's Summer School on International Children's Rights for directing me to this work.

3 In this context, all else being equal or *ceteris paribus* is highlighting that the tendency to believe other human beings at face value is observed in the absence of extraneous third variables such as personal dislike or idiosyncratic past experiences.

4 It is necessary to not overplay the effects of implicit bias. Although the idea of human behavior being more under the control of unconscious than conscious variables is titillating and has attracted significant research since Greenwald, McGhee and Schwartz's (1998) influential publication, recent meta-analytic studies have cast doubt on the magnitude of the effects associated with implicit variables (Oswald, Mitchell, Blanton, Jaccard, & Tetlock, 2013).

5 As an example, public health officials' COVID-19 response and recommendations have drawn serious criticism from medical doctors and children's advocates for failing to weigh the costs of lockdowns against the observed efficacy of such measures. Phoebe Southworth, June 10, 2021, *Lockdowns are 'the single biggest public health mistake in history', says top scientist, The Telegraph.* https://www.telegraph.co.uk/news/2021/06/10/lockdowns-single-biggest-public-health-mistake-history-says/

6 It is noteworthy that CASEL's philosophy appears to be relatively silent on children's rights. A search for 'children's human rights' on their site pulls up many materials but none that explicitly deals with how children's human rights are incorporated into their materials. It is necessary here to remind readers that human rights and equity concerns are not the same. Consequently, in using CASEL materials, there would have to be an active attempt to incorporate a children's human rights approach in the implementation of the program and assessments. This would likely involve modifying some of their materials.

References

Bill & Melinda Gates Foundation. (2012). *Asking students about teaching: Student perception surveys and their implementation.* Seattle, WA: Author.

Charlton, J.I. (1998). *Nothing about us without us: Disability oppression and empowerment.* Berkeley: University of California Press.

Conley, S., & Glasman, N.S. (2008). Fear, the school organization, and teacher evaluation. *Educational Policy*, 22(1), 63–85. https://doi.org/10.1177/0895904807311297

Covell, K., Howe, R.B., & Blokhuis, J.C. (2018). *The challenge of children's rights for Canada, Second edition.* Waterloo, ON: Wilfrid Laurier University Press.

Fricker, M. (2007). *Epistemic injustice: Power and the ethics of knowing.* Oxford: Oxford University Press.

Friedmann, L., & Covell, K. (2012). *Children's rights education.* www.childrensrightseducation.com.

Ginsberg, R., & Lyche, L.F. (2008). The culture of fear and the politics of education. *Educational Policy*, 22(1), 10–27. https://doi.org/10.1177/0895904807311293

Greenwald, A.G., McGhee, D.E., & Schwartz, J.L.K. (1998). Measuring individual differences in implicit cognition: The implicit association test. *Journal of Personality and Social Psychology*, 74(6), 1464–1480. https://doi.org/10.1037/0022-3514.74.6.1464

Grice, P. (1975). Logic and conversation. In P. Cole & J. Morgan (Eds.), *Syntax and semantics. Volume 3: Speech acts* (pp. 41–58). New York: Academic Press.

Hattie, J.A.C. (2003, October). Teachers make a difference: What is the research evidence? Paper presented at the Building Teacher Quality: What does the research tell us Australian Council for Education Research (ACER) Research Conference, Melbourne, Australia. Retrieved from http://research.acer.edu.au/research_conference_2003/4/

Hattie, J.A.C. (2009). *Visible learning: A synthesis of over 800 meta-analyses relating to achievement.* New York: Routledge.

Hughes, J.N., Wu, J.Y., Kwok, O.M., Villarreal, V., & Johnson, A.Y. (2012). Indirect effects of child reports of teacher-student relationship on achievement. *Journal of Educational Psychology*, 104(2), 350–365.

Kane, T.J., & Staiger, D.O. (2012). *Gathering feedback for teaching: Combining high-quality observations with student surveys and achievement gains* (Research Paper, MET Project). Seattle, WA: Bill & Melinda Gates Foundation.

Know Thy Impact: Teaching, Learning and Leading: An interview with John Hattie. (2013, Spring). *In Conversation*, Volume IV (Issue 2), 1–18. https://thelearningexchange.ca/wp-content/uploads/2017/04/Know-Thy-Impact-Teaching-Learning-and-Leading.pdf

Leighton, J.P. (2020). On barriers to accessing children's voices in school-based research. *Canadian Journal of Children's Rights*, 7(1), 164–193.

Leighton, J.P. (2022). Not all that counts is safe for counting: Barriers to collecting learning data for assessment purposes. In R. Lissitz & H. Jiao (Eds.), *Enhancing effective instruction and learning using assessment data* (pp. 187–213). Charlotte, NC: Information Age Publishing.

Leighton, J.P., & Sternberg, R.J. (2012). Reasoning and problem solving. In I. Weiner, A.F. Healy, & R.W. Proctor (Eds.), *Handbook of psychology*, Volume 4, Second Edition (pp. 631–659). New York: Wiley. https://doi.org/10.1002/9781118133880.hop204023

Malin, J.R., Brown, C., Ion, G., van Ackeren, I., Bremm, N., Luzmore, R., Flood, J., & Rind, G.M. (2020). World-wide barriers and enablers to achieving evidence-informed practice in education: What can be learnt from Spain, England, the United States, and Germany?. *Humanities and Social Sciences Communications*, 7, 99. https://doi.org/10.1057/s41599-020-00587-8

Norcross, J.C., & Lambert, M.J. (2018). Psychotherapy relationships that work III. *Psychotherapy*, 55(4), 303–315. http://dx.doi.org/10.1037/pst0000193

Nye, B., Konstantopoulos, S., & Hedges, L.V. (2004). How large are teacher effects? *Educational Evaluation and Policy Analysis*, 26(3), 237–257. https://doi.org/10.3102/01623737026003237

Oswald, F.L., Mitchell, G., Blanton, H., Jaccard, J., & Tetlock, P.E. (2013). Predicting ethnic and racial discrimination: A meta-analysis of IAT criterion studies. *Journal of Personality and Social Psychology*, 105(2), 171–192. https://doi.org/10.1037/a0032734

Rodham, H. (1973). Children under the law. *Harvard Educational Review*, 43(4), 487–514. https://doi.org/10.17763/haer.43.4.e14676283875773k

Soenens, B., Sierens, E., Vansteenkiste, M., Dochy, F., & Goossens, L. (2012). Psychologically controlling teaching: Examining outcomes, antecedents, and mediators. *Journal of Educational Psychology*, 104(1), 108–120. https://doi.org/10.1037/a0025742

Southworth, P. (2021, June 10, 2021). 'Lockdowns are 'the single biggest public health mistake in history', says top scientist.' *The Telegraph*. https://www.telegraph.co.uk/news/2021/06/10/lockdowns-single-biggest-public-health-mistake-history-says/

Strahan, D. B., & Poteat, B. (2020). Middle level students' perceptions of their social and emotional learning: An exploratory study. *RMLE Online*, 43(5), 1–15.

Thapa, A., Cohen, J., Guffey, S., & Higgins-D'Alessandro, A. (2013). A review of school climate research. *Review of Educational Research*, *83*(3), 357–385. https://doi.org/10.3102/0034654313483907

UN General Assembly (November 20, 1989). Convention on the Rights of the Child, United Nations, Treaty Series, vol. 1577, p. 3. Retrieved May 25, 2021 from www.refworld.org/docid/3ae6b38f0.html.

xSEL Labs (n.d.). *Data-informed social emotional learning instruction*. Retrieved July 21, 2021 from https://xsel-labs.com/resources/guide-to-data-informed-sel-instruction/

4
Keeping Your Eye on the Prize to Support Children

One of the most egregious mistakes educators make is getting stuck on certain teaching and assessment methods and losing track of the prize – watching children thrive in their learning. This should be the primary goal of whatever social and emotional program and/or assessment is used in the classroom. However, it is my view that educators and administrators can become obsessed with the latest innovation and technical know-how and lose sight of this primary goal. Aside from being dazzled by new learning programs, another distraction in the implementation of social and emotional programs is the misguided notion that sound assessments must always have high reliability coefficients, coupled with strong validity studies. This is simply not the case if the assessment is being used formatively to make low-stake decisions about learning, such as to monitor student progress and to yield on-the-fly information about how to tweak pedagogy and programming (Assessment Working Group, 2019). Therefore, it is necessary to keep the primary

DOI: 10.4324/9781003152781-4

goal in mind so as to not fall trap to illusory constraints that impede flexible design and use of assessments.

Assessments designed to measure children's social and emotional competencies should have a clear connection to children's learning. Moreover, assessments should be designed with students' input and suggestions, as well as involving children in evaluating the utility of the assessments and interpreting the data. For example, asking students about how they perceive the assessments and the information obtained from the assessments should be a subject of discussion to motivate their participation in the program.

Children's Voice in Social and Emotional Programming and Assessment

In applying any social and emotional program and assessment, children's responses to the initiative must be considered alongside administrative and/or pedagogical aims. Children are the supposed beneficiaries of the programs and assessments applied to them; thus, children should be consulted about their perceptions of the program and assessments that are or will be administered. They should also be invited to participate in child-friendly conversations about how the assessment data were interpreted and how the data are being used to modify programming. Consulting students for their perceptions and including them in data interpretation can enhance their comprehension and buy-in of programmatic goals. In other words, actively including children's voice and participation in social and emotional programming and assessment decisions can strengthen the effect of such initiatives.

The psychologist Edward Thorndike contributed greatly to the learning literature long ago by identifying the variables that influence *effects*. According to the APA's Dictionary of Psychology, Thorndike's law of effect can be understood as follows:

> ...if a response R produces a satisfying state of affairs (or a positive
> reinforcer), then an association is formed between R and the stimuli

> S present at the time R was made. As a result of this S—R association, R occurs whenever the organism encounters S. This part of the law of effect was the foundation of S—R theories of learning.

Collecting data in the form of children's responses (i.e., perceptions) about the social and emotional program and assessments they are about to experience (i.e., the stimulus) can help students create positive S-R associations. By including children's perspectives about the programming and assessments a teacher or school is considering for social and emotional development, children have the opportunity to feel relevant, respected and valued in their contribution to the goal. These feelings can be highly reinforcing for students. In the balance of this chapter, then, I expand on the concept of using assessments flexibly so that students can be meaningfully included in what is being administered to them. Toward this end, I elaborate on Clark McKown's (2019) meaningful measurement and supplement this concept with the much-needed perspective of children's rights.

McKown's Meaningful Measurement

It is beyond the scope of this book to include a detailed, step-by-step, technical outline of the procedures one can use to assess children's social and emotional readiness and wellness for learning. However, Clark McKown (2019) provides a highly practical manual on the steps required, including how to decide (1) the social and emotional competencies to focus on, (2) assessment goals and options (methods) to use, (3) interpretation and use of data and (4) strategies for including parents. When all four of these steps are considered, the concept of meaningful measurement is approximated because the measurement methods chosen are purposeful in helping to assess what has been decided is the goal for students. I do not have any objections to these particular four steps. However, my one objection is the omission of children's active voices in the process of applying these four steps. Thus, in this section, I add a children's rights perspective to each of these steps.

Step 1: Deciding the Social and Emotional Competencies on Which to Focus

McKown (2019) characterizes the task of deciding which social and emotional competencies to focus on as a *Tower of Babel* problem. There are a lot of different perspectives on social and emotional competencies. Some of the most influential perspectives come from comprehensive initiatives like CASEL, which was introduced earlier in the book in Chapter 1. Additional perspectives have emerged from research on (a) non-cognitive competencies including attitudes (e.g., mindsets) and social skills (Nagaoka, Farrington, Ehrlich & Heath, 2015), (b) 21st-century skills associated with cognitive, intrapersonal and interpersonal competencies (National Research Council, 2012) and (c) information-processing (Lemerise & Arsenio, 2000), neuropsychological functioning (Beauchamp & Anderson, 2010) and emotional skills (Halberstadt, Denham, & Dunsmore, 2001). Although all these perspectives present some listing of competencies, relatively little is said about the *principles* for why one particular type of program or assessment is in the best interest of children generally. This is not to say that specific programs do not matter, they do. But programs are simply tools, which should reflect broader principles. Principles matter for making revisions or tailoring programs to fit the needs of specific student populations and for aiding decision-making. Principles reflect fundamental values or propositions that undergird systems of belief, behavior and methods of thinking. Principles serve as useful controls or guard rails in a sea of possibilities.

The three principles that undergird this book were intentionally created to guide the selection of social and emotional competencies, and make revisions to programing and assessments as needed. Introduced in Chapter 1, these principles, at their core, reflect:

- The primacy of psychosocial wellness for students' learning (principle 1);
- The collection of assessment data in the service of students as rights holders (principle 2); and

- The student-teacher relationship and the trust that teachers engender as duty bearers (principle 3).

With these three principles, the decision to adopt specific social and emotional programs first requires conducting a *collaborative conversation about assessment goals*, one that involves children and their parents, of what intrapersonal (e.g., self-regulation) and interpersonal (e.g., empathy) attributes could help enhance children's readiness and wellness for learning. For example, in a school-wide approach or even in an individual classroom approach, the teacher can introduce stories about psychological wellness in learning, ask students what they think would help them learn using informal questions and surveys, organize small groups or games to explore the kinds of attributes that children require or want to acquire for learning, conduct one-to-one interviews with parents and students about what they think would improve the learning experience.

As indicated in Chapter 3, any social and emotional programmatic and assessment endeavor should begin by asking students to share what they think and feel about the prospect of incorporating a social and emotional initiative in the classroom. Instead of assuming what children think and/or feel from an adult perspective, this information should be actively sought from students. Collecting these data from students does not have to be complicated. It can involve simple, informal methods, such as the worksheet shown in Figure 4.1. Data such as these can be collected after the teacher has had an opportunity to *introduce the idea of emotions, feelings and interpersonal interactions and how they are related to learning.* Reading stories or watching videos can help younger children identify with fictional characters in a book or video, and launch a process of helping children explore and share their emotions and thoughts about specific learning situations (Leighton, 2019).

After discussing the possibility of a programmatic initiative and obtaining enthusiasm for its realization, the process of defining the most relevant social and emotional competencies on which to focus within the classroom can also be done collaboratively with students. By using the example materials introduced

MY NAME:

A JOURNEY OF WHAT HELPS ME LEARN

HOW DOES A GOOD LEARNER THINK AND ACT?

WHEN DO I FEEL MY BEST LEARNING?

WHAT ARE THE TOP 2 THINGS THAT MY TEACHER COULD DO DIFFERENTLY TO HELP ME LEARN?

1.
2.

WHEN DO I FEEL MY WORST LEARNING?

WHAT ARE THE TOP 3 THINGS THAT WOULD MAKE ME FEEL BETTER IN THE CLASSROOM?

1.
2.
3.

HOW CAN I HELP MY CLASSMATES LEARN?

Figure 4.1 Author designed example worksheet to gather preliminary data from students about social and emotional competencies related to learning. License owned by Author.

Defining Social and Emotional Readiness and Wellbeing	

We define social and emotional **readiness** as:

We define social and emotional **wellness** as:

Specific social and emotional **competencies/skills** that are included:

We **value** social and emotional **readiness** because_____

We **value** social and emotional **wellbeing** because _____

What specific competency do **we want to learn?**	Why is it **important to us?**	What behavior shows us this?	How **can it be assessed?**	How do **we resolve setbacks?**
1.				
2.				
3.				
4.				

Figure 4.2 Author generated illustration of Definition Worksheet modeled after xSEL Lab's worksheet (https://xsel-labs.com/resources/worksheets/). Icon on the right-hand corner is the symbol for the author's Learning Errors and Formative Feedback (LEAFF) model.

in Chapter 3, the process of collectively deciding what are the most critical social and emotional competencies to focus on can be done using something akin to the worksheet shown in Figure 4.2. The collective completion of this worksheet could be done with the class as a whole or by creating small groups of children working independently on specific problems that could be solved by introducing a social and emotional curriculum (e.g., enhancing orderliness in classroom discussions) and then coming together to share the discussions that occurred in the groups. The lesson here is to include children's voices and participation in all aspects of what is being done to them in the classroom. Incorporating children's voices from deciding the competencies that will be selected for development to the assessments that will be used to evaluate the program, gives them an opportunity to share what they consider to be in their best interest. It also begins to help students learn to give constructive feedback and speak up for themselves.

Recognition of children's readiness and wellness should be built into any program that aims to improve their social and emotional interactions; this includes recognizing their rights to voice and participation as a meaningful form of data. Teachers who recognize their role as duty bearers can build trust with students by including them in the process of deciding why the program might be beneficial, what it will involve and where are some sources of challenge. This is what principles buy in terms of narrowing the sea of possibilities.

In short, one always begins a social and emotional program by asking children and their parents about what they think *should be included* and how it *should be deployed*; only then will selection be in line with a children's rights approach.

Although I have not elaborated on parental discourse, parental consultation could include teacher-parent meetings, newsletters, town halls and/or any other form of collaborative communication designed to gather feedback (see McKown, 2019 for more information). Of course, once meaningful consultation with children and parents is carried out and the data are reviewed, an off-the-shelf or proprietary program can be selected. But, importantly, the program and its assessments should be modified as required to fit the context and needs of the students involved. The program and assessments need to be tailored to the students, not the other way around. McKown states correctly that feeling a little unsure about the process of deciding what to focus on is part of the process. McKown (2019) indicates "the struggle is an important part of coming to clarity and committing, together, to what will be the district's focus" (p. 15). The one aspect of this quote I would revise, however, is that it is not the district's focus; it is also the focus of the children and the parents, which the district is serving. There will be opportunity for refining, evaluation and revision, but always with children's and parental input.

Step 2: Assessment Goals and Methods

Once the social and emotional competencies have been selected and defined, the next step is to decide on the over-arching assessment goals and methods for measuring the social and emotional competencies of interest. Satisfying these goals with appropriate methods requires the creation of sub-goals such as the *type of data* or information the assessment should yield. Toward this end, it is necessary to recognize that there are many assessment formats that yield different data at different levels of rigor. One way to begin to categorize assessments formats is to first divide them by whether they are administered *during a program* or *after a program* of studies is completed. Depending on when assessments are administered, the assessment will meet different goals. For example, *formative assessments* are typically administered during a program of studies. Formative assessments are designed with the goal of measuring what aspects of the learning objectives students are struggling to learn in order to inform the modification of teachers' instruction to better help the students acquire the skills of interest. Formative assessments often play a crucial role in meeting the goal of *progress monitoring*, namely, the repeated measurement of competencies to see how well students are responding to a given intervention. When considering social and emotional competencies, the intervention is the social and emotional program administered, and formative assessments can be used to monitor how well students are learning the specific competencies of interest. Using assessments to monitor a child's progress fits well within a child's rights approach because the routine collection of data offers students an opportunity to voice their concerns, likes and dislikes. In essence, routine data collection can be used to include them and their voices in the process of actively providing feedback and using their feedback to revise aspects of the program delivery.

In contrast, *summative assessments* are designed with the goal of measuring the mastery of learning objectives at the end of a given program of study; often numerical or letter rankings are assigned to individual performance. It is my view that summative assessments *should not* play a major role in social and emotional programming aside from providing teachers and school leaders with a final source of data for evaluating how well a specific program has led to desired growth or overall changes in a group of children. Summative assessments do not lend themselves to meeting the goals of measuring individual social and emotional competencies. This is because summative assessments are designed to measure the correctness of a given response or achievement of a specific target skill. However, there is no obvious correct response in situations that require social and emotional competencies, and no final target; certainly not if individual and/or cultural variables are considered. Indeed, neither the school nor the teacher should be *parenting the child* in the form of nudging the child to acquire a specific form of social and emotional character. This is a parental task and teachers and school systems would be overstepping their role by imposing an outcome-based education of social and emotional competencies.

Unlike cognitive skills, such as mathematical knowledge, or even writing skills, where one can evaluate performance with some agreed-upon objectivity, it would be foolish to think that the same applies to inherently dynamic competencies such as self-regulation, empathy, time management skills and many other types of intra- and inter-personal social and emotional attributes. In fact, the working premise that there are correct and incorrect social and emotional competencies is detrimental to children who happen to present diverse ways of acting or thinking, or feeling (Hoffman, 2009). While all children may benefit from learning to self-regulate, it is necessary to recognize that there are variations in self-regulation. Children's behavior reflects a mixture of both biologically based temperament and culturally enhanced experiences. Thus, comparing students in their acquisition of social and emotional competencies to a norm or expecting that they meet specific targets does not make developmental or psychological sense in my view – especially in light of either cultural diversity or a children's rights approach. Nonetheless, summative assessments can provide data for the purpose of *program evaluation* to show group trends longitudinally. For example, if pre-program and post-program assessments are administered to measure the competencies of interest in different student groups, a group comparison of performance may provide a rough measure of children's overall change in a given direction over time and with multiple cohorts. However, without a control group, any measured change in students' overall performance cannot be attributed to the social and emotional program implemented (Cook & Campbell, 1979).

I propose that the best type of assessments to use for social and emotional programs is formative assessments. These assessments should be administered for the purpose of progress monitoring as mentioned previously, and as a way to *continually improve* students' experiences of the social and emotional program administered. Formative assessments can facilitate the goals of the program, and ultimately curricular learning objectives. The end goal of a successful social and emotional program should not be a report card mark or grade but, rather, the support of students' readiness to learn and wellbeing. These assessments should be inclusive of children's voices in the improvement of the assessments for measuring the relationships students experience towards successful classroom learning. For example, the assessments should include questions such as whether their intrinsic motivation for learning mathematics has improved, whether they feel more attentive during social studies projects and/or whether they feel more confident about identifying what they are having trouble learning. In addition to formative assessment data, teachers and school leaders can also look to other types of data such as completion of homework, logged study time, achievement performance, time on task, attendance and other behavioral indicators of whether students are increasingly successful in their learning.

The measurement of social and emotional competencies is in its infancy. In fact, citing a recent study by Jagers, Rivas-Drake and Borowski (2018), the Assessment Work Group (2019) concluded that the "field has not yet realized [a] vision" (p. 33) that could be used to reduce racial inequity and oppression. What this means is that researchers and program developers do not yet know how to realize a vision of reducing or at least not perpetuating gender or cultural stereotypes. For these reasons, there needs to be caution in how certain competencies such as emotional self-regulation or conflict resolution is differentially modeled for children. There is no one size fits all. For example, some girls could actually be supported in learning how to better express their anger directly during conflicts instead of relationally by marginalizing members of their peer group, while some boys might be supported in learning how to express anger less physically.

Thus, given the nature of social and emotional constructs, namely, that there is *no universal consensus for targets of mastery*, and that children have biologically based temperaments and culturally influenced experiences, grading these assessments is unjustifiable at the present time. Numerical rankings or grades should be entirely avoided with students. Social and emotional assessment data should be collected and used only to generate discussion with children one-to-one or, if appropriate, in a group or small peer-group setting. Using formative assessment results to lead discussions of whether a given assessment result captured the essence of the competency being measured, and what variables may be facilitating or hindering attainment of a given competency can be more productive for student development than to assign scores.

Once assessment goals are selected, the particular methods for generating data need to be considered. According to the Assessment Work Group (2019), there are many methods or approaches that can be used to meet the goals of social and emotional assessment. For example, shown in Table 4.1 is a list of assessment methods. If the over-arching goal is formative and there is commitment to including children's participation and voice in assessment data, three of the six methods listed in Table 4.1 are preferred. The three that permit teachers to meet formative assessment goals are: self-reports, observation rating scales and administrative records. Before elaborating on the reasons for using self-reports, observation rating scales and administrative records to meet formative assessment goals, I explain the reasons direct assessment, standards-based assessment and report cards do not.

Direct assessment, standards-based assessment and report cards are not recommended in the measurement of social and emotional competencies because these assessment methods generally involve little input from children. These methods are largely *outcome*-focused and therefore reflect the assumption

Table 4.1 Summary of Methods for Measuring Social and Emotional Competencies (see Assessment Work Group, 2019)

Summary of Methods for Measuring Social and Emotional Competencies			
Assessment Form	*Main Strengths*	*Main Limitations*	*Constructs*
1. Self-report	Simple, feasible	Vulnerable to respondent biases	Beliefs, attitudes and dispositions
2. Observation rating scales	Simple, feasible	Vulnerable to rater (teacher) biases, time-consuming to carry out for each student	Observable behaviors
3. Direct assessment	Objective measure of skills	Costly to develop	Thinking skills and knowledge
4. Standards-based assessment	Linked to standards or targets, can be integrated with instruction, outcome-focused	Not straightforward to create, no widely available system	Current mastery of competencies
5. Report card	Widely used, typically includes behavioral descriptors	Parent concerns about including social and emotional competencies alongside curricular objectives (permanent information attached to child)	Overall mastery of competencies
6. Administrative records	Ease of availability (e.g., attendance, punctuality, completion, participation)	Proxies for competencies	Impact (or effect) of competencies

that social and emotional constructs or targets can be objectively assessed; in other words, there is an obvious end-point to social and emotional learning. As I mentioned previously, the measurement of social and emotional competencies is not at a level of sophistication that would warrant this level of trust in the targets of measurement. Moreover, I highly doubt that social and emotional competencies will ever become associated with unequivocal measures as long as cultural and human diversity are recognized and valued. Thus, methods such as direct assessments, standards-based assessments and report cards are better suited for measuring uniquely specified cognitive skills than social and emotional competencies.

In contrast, self-reports, observation rating scales and administrative records are better suited to providing ongoing information about student performance. First, these assessment tools can be modified depending on specific situations. For example, self-report surveys can be modified by deleting irrelevant items or adding items that specifically focus on details of interventions. If conflict resolution is a focus in the classroom, additional items can be generated to obtain more data about this focal aspect of the intervention. Importantly, self-reports can be more easily adapted to include children's feedback in the modification of the instrument. Although self-reports are susceptible to response bias, there are ways to minimize this bias by asking questions from different perspectives and using alternate forms of delivery. For example, a survey item that asks students directly about whether they *trust a teacher* may be too susceptible to positive response bias. Instead, items that ask students about whether they feel comfortable seeking feedback from the teacher, or telling the teacher if something is not working well in their learning environment can probe students about whether they feel heard or protected by a teacher.

Likewise, observation rating scales can be modified to have items focus on what has been considered to be most relevant in the teaching and assessment of social and emotional competencies (e.g., controlled discussion, turn-taking, being mindful of quiet time for others to complete their work). An advantage of observation rating scales is that they require raters to look for behavioral indicators of constructs and, thus, avoid participants' response bias. For example, if the classroom is focused on conflict resolution, observational rating scales encourage teachers and students to identify the behaviors that show positive versus negative conflict resolution. Behaviors such as identifying the problem, bringing the affected parties together for discussion, allowing relevant parties to have a turn at presenting their side of the story, practicing perspective-taking, brainstorming solutions and evaluating whether a proposed solution addresses the original problem can be included in rating checklists. When the observation of behaviors is added to the measurement of self-reported beliefs and attitudes, evidence is generated from different sources and can facilitate informed inferences about the success of interventions and programs for students, including how to modify them as they are being implemented. This has been successfully done in the MET project (Kane & Staiger, 2012). Likewise, administrative records can serve to supplement data about children's social and emotional competencies. For example, data that reflect students' regular attendance and improved grades can lend support to inferences that a child is feeling welcomed at school and feels greater interest in the academic lessons presented at school. Children who are getting their learning needs met in the classroom are typically going to perform better than those who are not.

Step 3: Interpretation and Use of Data

Once the assessment goals and methods have been defined and applied, respectively, the next step requires a principled approach to interpreting and using formative assessment data. McKown (2019) describes a straightforward plan for interpreting and using data. McKown (2019, p. 68) describes four essential stages in interpretation and use:

1. A team is identified that is charged with collating and preparing the data for review. This stage should ensure that the team is composed of members who are genuinely qualified to make sense of the data. For example, team members

should have familiarity with the student population, teaching and assessment methods and social and emotional development. The experience and qualifications of the team are relevant because these are the individuals who will be deciding how results are reported and what any "scores" might mean.

2. Once the team is identified, the team reviews the data and develops a first-pass at an interpretation of what the data indicate. In other words, the team is charged with putting together a reasoned case for what the data say about the social and emotional competencies of the students, and what should be done with the results.

3. Based on this first-pass at interpretation, the team should be able to show a reasoned case for the following three objectives:
   - ○ What does the data indicate about students' strengths and needs?
   - ○ What are the actions to be taken to support students' strengths and address their needs?
   - ○ What is the implementation plan, including timelines, for doing something with the results?
     Depending on the level of consensus achieved in the interpretation of the data, the team may need to reconvene repeatedly for further discussion to reach agreement about the interpretation and use of the data.

4. Upon consensus, the team executes a plan for using the data.

The reasoning underlying McKown's stages is relatively clear. In fact, its overall structure could be adopted in many situations with some modifications.

I propose the following modifications based on a child rights approach to the assessment of social and emotional competencies: First, formative assessment data *should not lead to individual scores* that are reported to children or parents. Formative assessment data should inform program monitoring and strengthening but should not provide any semblance of a summative evaluation. Providing scores to students and/or parents runs the risk of having scores misinterpreted and also runs the risk of leading to the labeling of children. This is unnecessary and potentially harmful as the scores are not diagnostic. Second, *the expertise of the team* is more important than the size of the team. Thus, the team can be small and involve a select group of 2–3 teachers from adjacent grades (e.g., Grades 1 and 2), who have the requisite knowledge of the students being assessed. The team may be kept small for several reasons. If the team becomes too large, then scheduling and discussions become challenging, and teams may be less motivated to meet. Also, if the data are treated as formative, and as a way to monitor program progress and tweak the program where it is needed, then the stakes of the assessment are low. Thus, the team can be more agile in making the results actionable. If a school has a counselor or psychologist on site, counselors and/or psychologists can provide additional guidance in linking the results to the design of an action plan for strengthening students' social and emotional program development.

There is a benefit to working with low-stakes, formative assessment data. One of the main benefits is that low-stakes formative assessment data provide greater flexibility in data interpretation and use. The Assessment Work Group (2019) of which McKown was a part, indicates this important point:

> Observing a student's behavior in the flow of instruction and adjusting teaching style is low-stakes. The time period is limited, and the consequences of the decision are low. Informal assessment with minimal evidence of psychometric merit is, in this context, appropriate. In fact, teachers constantly evaluate students informally to adjust their teaching.
>
> (p. 36)

Recognizing that formative assessment data can be collected and used without having to observe a high standard of psychometric rigor is necessary to be able to collect data continuously from students and to be able to modify aspects of interventions and/or programs as required based on the data. If a high level of psychometric rigor were required for every instrument used to collect formative assessment data and inform instruction on the fly, the utility of the data would quickly disappear because it would take too long to confirm the precision of the instruments and next to impossible to make modifications to the instruments. Teachers need the freedom to collect formative assessment data as often as required to adjust or tweak social and emotional programs based on what they (or the team) understand the data to reveal.

In an effort to increase basic understanding of assessment uses, the Assessment Work Group (2019) outlines the relationships between the intended purpose of an assessment, its evaluative questions (i.e., the questions the assessment is designed to answer), the evidence required to make valid inferences from the assessment data and ultimately the score metric that is produced from the assessment. I have elaborated and added to these relationships as shown in Tables 4.2 and 4.3.

By examining Tables 4.2 and 4.3, it becomes clear that different assessments require different levels of psychometric evidence for their use. This is one reason to stay away from any summative assessment that involves assigning scores to children for their social and emotional competencies. At the present time, there is insufficient evidence about the nature of social and emotional constructs and their measurement to warrant summative assessments and the use of scores. Although high internal consistency values could be estimated to provide a preliminary level of assurance that something stable is being measured, this is only a narrow index of what is required to have any confidence in scores and in making valid inferences about what the scores mean for students. A high internal consistency value for a self-report survey simply means that item responses correlate highly with each other; thus, providing some evidence that whatever competency is being measured, it is stable and similar across all the items or questions included in the survey. However, this is by far not the only issue to consider in having confidence in scores. Other issues include the manner in which the social and emotional competency has been defined (i.e., the construct), and how well it is reflected by the items included in the assessment. If the description of the competency is narrow, then many features of the competency will be missing and may not accurately describe the competency as it is typically interpreted by

Table 4.2 Modification and Elaboration of Relationship between Assessment Goals, and Criteria for Using Assessment for Meeting Goals: High Stakes Situations as Outlined by Assessment Work Group (2019)

Relationship between Assessment Goals, and Criteria for Using Assessment for Meeting Goals: High Stakes Situations

Intended Use (Goals)	Evaluative Question Underlying Assessment	Rigor of Evidence	Stability of Metrics
1. I want to formally infer how my students compare to the general population.	How well does the normative sample reflect the group I care about? How current are norms?	Look at the characteristics of the normative sample and timeframe of normative data collection.	The higher stakes the decision, the better quality the norming sample ought to be.
2. I want to formally understand student strengths and needs and needs to help guide my instruction. And assign scores to their performance.	Does the assessment measure competencies taught? Can assessment scores guide instruction? Is assessment score associated with the competencies taught?	Look at the relationship between assessment score skills and curriculum content. You will need to calculate score reliability and correlations with other related competencies.	If students will be assigned scores based on assessment content, then internal consistency should be calculated. The temporal stability of scores needs to be checked. Correlate scores with other variables.

3. I want to formally evaluate student progress over time. And assign scores to their performance.	Can the assessment detect a change in a student's skill level over time? What level of change are you expecting to see?	Look at the evidence that scores increase with age and learning. The evidence should show the consistency of performance on repeated assessments.	If students will be assigned scores based on performance, then scores need to show improvements by age/ learning with cross-sectional or longitudinal data. Test-retest reliability should also be included in the assessment.
4. I want to formally evaluate the program being implemented.	Are the assessments sensitive to the intended program effects? Is the assessment designed to measure what the program teaches?	Look at evidence associated with formally understanding student strengths and needs, and how it helps with instruction (#2). Look at evidence of how the new instruction students have been exposed to compares to a control group. Requires experimental design, which is often unfeasible to do in school settings.	If students will be assigned scores based on assessment content, then internal consistency should be calculated. Temporal stability of scores needs to be checked. Correlate scores with other variables. The metrics to evaluate are the size of the correlation between school quality and assessment scores. Moreover, evidence of higher performance in the treatment group versus the control group should be examined.

Table 4.3 Modification and Elaboration of Relationship between Assessment Goals, and Criteria for Using Assessment for Meeting Goals: Low Stakes Situations as Outlined by Assessment Work Group (2019)

Relationship between Assessment Goals, and Criteria for Using Assessment for Meeting Goals: Low Stakes Situations

Intended Use (Goals)	Evaluative Question Underlying Assessment	Rigor of Evidence	Stability of Metrics
5. I want to engage in the continuous improvement of my teaching.	Does performance on the assessment reflect the skills of the students and the quality of their practices?	Look at the associations or correlations between school quality and student competence in longitudinal, quasi-experimental, or experimental designs. The most likely source of evidence will be to gather assessment data over time and see whether overall classroom scores improve. The feasibility of experimental designs in school settings is generally low.	If students will not be assigned any scores, then the assessments do not have to achieve a high standard of internal consistency because no individual level student inferences will be made. Only group data will be used. The metrics to evaluate are the size of the correlation between school quality and assessment scores. Evidence that continuous improvement leads to improved scores.

6. I want to informally evaluate student progress over time and improve my teaching. But I do not want to assign scores to students.	Does performance on the assessment reflect the skills of the students and the quality of their practices?	Look at the associations or correlations between student performance and observational ratings of their behaviors in class and administrative records. Compare student performance with what students indicate in interviews with you when you ask them about their responses. Seek additional information about student responses as a whole by discussing the assessment with the class.	If students will not be assigned scores, then the assessments do not have to achieve a high standard of internal consistency because no individual-level student inferences will be made. Only group data are being used to inform the progress of a program over time and whether students are experiencing the program as expected.

individuals, including parents and students. An example may be useful here.

Consider the self-report survey shown in Table 4.4, designed to measure four competencies in elementary school children: self-control (SC), persistence (p), mastery-orientation (MO) and academic self-efficacy (ASE). A teacher survey also measures students' self-control, persistence and social competence (SoC)

Table 4.4 Elementary School Student Survey of Four Social and Emotional Competencies

Thank you for taking the time to answer these questions. This is NOT A TEST. There are no right or wrong answers. Please be honest when answering the questions. Your honest answers will help your school or program do a better job to help you learn! These questions are about different ways students may behave in school. Please mark the box that best describes you.

Question	Not at All Like Me	A Little Like Me	Somewhat Like Me	A Lot Like Me
1. I can wait in line patiently (SC)				
2. I sit still when I'm supposed to. (SC)				
3. I can wait for my turn to talk in class. (SC)				
4. I can easily calm down when excited. (SC)				
5. I calm down quickly when I get upset. (SC)				
6. I can do even the hardest homework if I try. (ASE)				
7. I can learn the things taught in school. (ASE)				
8. I can figure out difficult homework. (ASE)				

Table 4.4 (continued)

Question	Not at All Like Me	A Little Like Me	Somewhat Like Me	A Lot Like Me

These next questions are about how you get your schoolwork done. Mark the box that best describes you.

9. If I solve a problem wrong the first time, I just keep trying until I get it right. (P)

10. When I do badly on a test, I work harder the next time. (P)

11. I always work hard to complete my school work. (P)

The last set of questions will ask you how you feel about school. Please mark the box that best describes you.

12. I do my schoolwork because I like to learn new things. (MO)

13. I do my schoolwork because I'm interested in it. (MO)

14. I do my schoolwork because I enjoy it. (MO)

(see Table 4.5). These surveys are taken from the Child Trends 2014 document titled *Measuring Elementary School Students' Social and Emotional Skills: Providing Educators with Tools to Measure and Monitor Social and Emotional Skills that Lead to Academic Success*. Child Trends (childtrends.org) is a leading organization working on enhancing the lives of children and youth so their surveys serve as a valuable example. A sample of their student survey is also featured in the 2017 publication from the Kansas State Department of Education, *Measuring Social-Emotional Character Growth Toolkit*. The four competencies of interest (i.e., constructs) are defined as follows (Child Trends, 2014, p. 34):

Table 4.5 Elementary School Teacher Survey of Three Social and Emotional Competencies

Please think about the student's behavior in the last QUARTER or SINCE the last reporting period. If this is the first report of the year/program, think about the student's behavior since she or he has been in your class.
On a scale from 1 to 4, how well do each of the statements describe the student's behavior? Would you say 1-NONE OF THE TIME, 2-A LITTLE OF THE TIME, 3-MOST OF THE TIME, or 4-ALL OF THE TIME?

Question	None of the Time	A Little of the Time	Most of the Time	All of the Time
1. Worked on tasks until they were finished. (P)	1	2	3	4
2. Kept working on an activity that was difficult. (P)	1	2	3	4
3. Waited in line patiently. (SC)	1	2	3	4
4. Sat still when he/she was supposed to. (SC)	1	2	3	4
5. Waited for what he/she wanted. (SC)	1	2	3	4
6. Focused on tasks until they were finished. (P)	1	2	3	4
7. Worked well with peers. (SoC)	1	2	3	4
8. Resolved problems with peers without becoming aggressive. (SoC)	1	2	3	4
9. Was thoughtful of the feelings of her/his peers. (SoC)	1	2	3	4
10. Cooperated with peers without prompting. (SoC)	1	2	3	4

Table 4.5 (continued)

Question	None of the Time	A Little of the Time	Most of the Time	All of the Time
11. Understood the feelings of his/her own peers. (SoC)	1	2	3	4
12. Resolved problems with peers on his/her own. (SoC)	1	2	3	4

- Self-control (SC) involves the student having the ability to: (a) control emotions and behavior, (b) inhibit negative behavior, (c) sustain attention or concentrate on a given task and (d) wait for his or her turn or for what he or she wants.

- Persistence (P) involves the student choosing to continue toward a goal in spite of obstacles, difficulties, or discouragement. For persistence to be present, a student's actions must be voluntary and indicate an underlying determination to continue at a task or goal despite challenges of failure that may occur along the way.

- Mastery orientation (MO) involves a student's desire to complete work in order to learn and improve his or her skills and ability rather than for external validation (e.g., wanting to look good in front of peers and teachers; get good grades).

- Academic self-efficacy (ASE) involves a student's belief that he or she can effectively perform a variety of academic tasks.

- Social competence (SoC) involves a student having the ability to: (a) understand and take peers' perspectives (e.g., by picturing what peers are feeling or thinking), (b) work well with peers to accomplish a task, (c) resolve problems in ways that maximize positive consequences and minimizes negative consequences for oneself and one's peers and (d) behave appropriately according to the situation or social norms.

It is important to note that only four competencies are measured in the student survey, namely, self-control, persistence, mastery orientation and academic self-efficacy. Students' social competence is measured by teachers who complete a survey designed to also rate individual students on self-control and persistence. Thus, the social competence of children is only measured by their teachers.

Most of the internal consistency values for the seven sections of the student and teacher survey are reported to be above .70, suggesting an acceptable level of structure for these measured constructs (Nunnally, 1978). The two exceptions include the self-control and academic self-efficacy sections. First, the self-control section of the student survey did not yield a value because three of the items were deemed to be measuring *emotional self-regulation* and not self-control. The rationale for judging that these three items were measuring emotional self-regulation instead of self-control is unclear, however. This is because the definition of self-control put forth in the document could well include emotional self-regulation; thus, the definition is sufficiently broad to include these items. Moreover, failure to calculate an internal consistency value based on this exclusion undermines the definition of the construct. A related problem with failing to calculate internal consistency for self-control is that a self-control *score* is subsequently produced, which now includes items on emotional self-regulation. It is therefore ambiguous how this score is supposed to be interpreted. The basic problem is not that there are different items included in the student survey of self-control; the problem is that when different items are included, and a self-control score is produced, we need evidence of the psychometric structure that undergirds the survey to interpret the score. Second, the internal consistency value for the academic self-efficacy section of the survey was reported at .65, just below .70. Given that this section of the student survey only included three items, a value of .65 is acceptable in my view. But the more substantive issue is what does an aggregated score on academic-self efficacy mean for a student? I would argue that the score does not convey much information to students.

The reason for highlighting these surveys is to show the types of assessments that are used alongside practices that could and should be eliminated to make the process easier and better for teachers and students. First, these surveys are acceptable forms of gathering data from students. However, as already mentioned in previous sections, there is no obvious need or rationale to provide students with survey scores. In fact, providing students with scores is somewhat misleading as the survey indicates in its instructions that there are *no right or wrong answers.* The survey instructions are correct given what we know about social and emotional competencies; there are no right or wrong answers because people have different temperaments and cultural backgrounds. Moreover, social and emotional competencies are developed and mastered at different rates and over long-term time frames. Hence, any meaning attached to a score at a given time to make a judgment about a student is potentially invalid and unreliable. Withholding scores from students is therefore recommended because students will often perceive scores as "marks" or "grades." Students will begin to think that there are correct or better answers to these assessments. To not confuse students or facilitate the misuse of scores, then, every effort should be made to not provide individual scores but, instead, discuss the results with the class and what they mean for the program.

If scores are calculated for teachers' use, internal consistency values should be estimated for all sections of the student survey, and sections that reflect distinct competencies should not be aggregated unless there is a strong rationale to do so. The same holds true for sections of the teacher survey. The teacher ratings or scores should not be communicated to students even if only for information. The aggregated ratings for students via their self-report survey and the teacher's ratings should be kept by the teacher in confidence and discussed with the team that is facilitating the implementation of the social and emotional program. The ratings can be used to monitor an overall class response to the program, including how well they like or dislike the program, tweak the program, or even pay attention to specific competencies with which some students may be struggling.

It is because there are no correct answers in social and emotional functioning that summative assessments and/or formative assessment scores are meaningless. There are simply too many ambiguities with the definition and measurement of social and emotional competencies to pretend we can provide children with scores related to competencies. Moreover, teachers need to be highly aware that attaching too much significance to such scores is unwarranted. Not only because of the fluid nature of social and emotional competencies but also because teachers are doing the ratings; so, they are subject to bias in the way they may be perceiving their students. Teachers need to be aware of the potential biases that exist in rating students.

Step 4: Strategies for Including Parents and Children

Adopting a child rights approach to social and emotional programs and assessments means including children's perspectives from the start, and being mindful to engage in practices that are designed in their best interest. Thus, the design and implementation of social and emotional programming must be done with students' and also parents' input.

Including parents is necessary because they are the primary individuals responsible for educating and raising their children. Thus, parents will have insights about their children that can help teachers become aware of children's cultural backgrounds and experiences. When schools and teachers begin to instruct children on ways to handle their emotions, get along with others and think about themselves, this is no longer about teaching basic skills in math or science. Teaching children about how to monitor their emotions and respond to conflict can be viewed as stepping into the realm of what parents and caregivers are often expected to do. Moreover, especially in situations where school demographics are diverse, it is necessary to recognize that certain aspects of the social and emotional programming may not be welcomed by parents, not simply because the competencies may be up for debate, but because it is perceived to be an affront to their role as parents to not have been consulted. A cultural example may be useful here. The example involves language and the use of the term *Latinx*. Some teachers and school administrators may believe that removing the gendered aspect of the term Latino and/or Latina by inserting an 'x' at the end of each term is a way to respect Latin culture. However, this tinkering with the gendered nature of Latin culture and language can be perceived as offensive by members of Latin communities who embrace the gendered aspects of their cultural language.

Strategies for including children and parents should begin at the same time that a school or teacher decides to begin a social and emotional program and assessment initiative. The school, including the teacher, should not only share the intent and examples of programs with children and parents but also be open to modifying the program and assessments depending on what children and parents have to say. Formal consultation should include information in newsletters, websites, links to example programs, town hall discussions and individual one-to-one sessions and a transparent working plan for how children and parents will be involved in decisions of construct definition, implementation and evaluation. In addition, children and parents should be consulted on the selection of the team members who will be charged with reviewing any assessment data and proposing actions that are taken in light of the data. Although not all parents may wish to be involved, meaningful and respectful consultation with parents and inclusion of children will increase buy in of the goals of the social and emotional program and assessments administered.

On a final note, McKown (2019) addresses the issue of parent discomfort and how teachers and school administrators can tackle the necessary consultative processes. One of the big issues McKown notes is explaining to parents how assessment data will be used. Parents may worry that assessment scores will be used to label or diagnose the child or that assessment scores will be formally recorded and "follow the child" throughout his or her school trajectory. These are not trivial concerns. Parental concerns will be much less of a barrier to social and emotional initiatives if parents are consulted early and if teachers and schools avoid using assessment scores in any individual way other than for overall classroom information. Assessment results can be misused precisely because the collection of numerical information often gives the appearance of exactitude. This can be dangerous for children and their parents especially given that the tools used to generate these data are experimental at best even if proprietary programs are selected. If the goal of assessing social and emotional competencies is done to genuinely learn about students and help them succeed in the classroom, the most effective use of the data is to provide a continuous flow of feedback from students about how teachers can better structure and facilitate learning opportunities and interactions within the classroom.

Summary of Five Key Points

In this chapter, five key points were made. These include the following:

- Collecting data in the form of children's responses (i.e., perceptions) about the social and emotional program and assessments they are about to experience (i.e., the stimulus) can help students create positive S-R associations. By including children's perspectives about the programming and assessments a teacher or school is considering for social and emotional development, children have the opportunity to feel relevant, respected and valued in their contribution to the goal.
- Although Clark McKown (2019) provides a highly practical manual on the four steps required to collect data from children (i.e., the social and emotional competencies to focus on, assessment goals and options (methods) to use, interpretation and use of data and strategies for including parents), the one missing element in each of these steps is the elevated role of the child. The child's participation should contribute not only to the provision of data but also to decisions and interpretations of assessment data.
- When considering social and emotional competencies, the intervention is the social and emotional program administered, and formative assessments provide a better approach to monitoring how well students are learning the specific

competencies of interest. Using assessments to monitor a child's progress fits well within a child's rights approach because the routine collection of data offers students an opportunity to voice their concerns, likes and dislikes.

- Although formative assessment data should be collected, the data *should not lead to individual scores* that are reported to children or parents. Formative assessment data should inform program monitoring and strengthening but should not provide any semblance of a summative evaluation. Providing scores to students and/or parents runs the risk of having scores misinterpreted and also runs the risk of leading to the labeling of children.

- Providing students with survey scores on their social and emotional competencies is misleading as there are *no right or wrong answers.* People deploy different social and emotional responses depending on the demands of distinct situations. Children have different temperaments and cultural backgrounds that can lead to manners of responding. Moreover, social and emotional competencies are developed and mastered at different rates and over long-term time frames.

References

American Psychological Association. (n.d.). Law of effect. In *APA dictionary of psychology.* Retrieved August 1, 2021 from https://dictionary.apa.org/law-of-effect.

Assessment Work Group. (2019). *Student social and emotional competence assessment: The current state of the field and a vision for its future.* Chicago, IL: Collaborative for Academic, Social, and Emotional Learning (CASEL). Retrieved on June 1, 2021 from https://casel.org/wp-content/uploads/2020/04/AWG-State-of-the-Field-Report_2019_DIGITAL_Final.pdf.

Beauchamp, M.H., & Anderson, V. (2010). SOCIAL: An integrative framework for the development of social skills. *Psychological Bulletin, 136*(1), 39–64. https://doi.org/10.1037/a0017768

Child Trends. (July, 2014). *Measuring elementary school students' social and emotional skills: Providing educators with tools to measure and monitor social and emotional skills that lead to academic success.* Bethesda, MD: Author. Retrieved on June 19, 2021 from https://www.childtrends.org/wp-content/uploads/2014/08/2014-37CombinedMeasuresApproachandTablepdf1.pdf.

Cook, T.D., & Campbell, D.T. (1979). *Quasi- experimentation: Design and analysis issues for field settings.* Chicago, IL: Rand-McNally.

Halberstadt, A.G., Denham, S.A., & Dunsmore, J.C. (2001). Affective social competence. *Social Development, 10*(1), 79–119. https://doi.org/10.1111/1467-9507.00150

Hoffman, D.M. (2009). Reflecting on social emotional learning: A critical perspective on trends in the United States. *Review of Educational Research, 79*(2), 533–556. https://doi.org/10.3102/0034654308325184

Jagers, R., Rivas-Drake, D., and Borowski, T. (2018). *Equity and social and emotional learning: A cultural analysis.* Collaborative for Academic, Social and Emotional Learning (CASEL) Retrieved June 2, 2021 from https://measuringsel.casel.org/wp-content/uploads/2018/11/Frameworks-Equity.pdf.

Kane, T.J., & Staiger, D.O. (2012). *Gathering feedback for teaching: Combining high-quality observations with student surveys and achievement gains* (Research Paper, MET Project). Seattle, WA: Bill & Melinda Gates Foundation.

Leighton, J.P. (2019). Students' interpretation of formative feedback: Three claims for why we know so little about something so important. *Journal of Educational Measurement (Special Issue on Classroom Assessment), 56*, 793–814. https://doi.org/10.1111

Lemerise, E.A., & Arsenio, W.F. (2000). An integrated model of emotion processes and cognition in social information processing. *Child Development, 71*(1), 107–118. https://doi.org/10.1111/1467-8624.00124

McKown, C. (2019). *Assessing students' social and emotional learning: A guide to meaningful measurement (SEL solution series).* New York: Norton Professional Books.

Nagaoka, J., Farrington, C., Ehrlich, S., & Heath, R. (2015). Foundations for young adult success: A developmental framework. *The University of Chicago Consortium on Chicago School Research.* https://doi.org/10.13140/RG.2.2.28780.26247.

National Research Council. (2012). *Education for Life and Work: Developing Transferable Knowledge and Skills in the 21st Century.* Retrieved from: https://www.nap.edu/catalog/13398/education-for-life-and-work-developing-transferable-knowledge-and-skills.

Nunnally, J.C. (1978). *Psychometric theory.* 2nd Edition. New York: McGraw-Hill.

5

The Assessment Elephant in the Room: When Societies Discount Children

The assessment of children's social and emotional readiness and wellbeing must consider the broader environment in which children are living. I began this book with Bronfenbrenner's Bioecological model (Bronfenbrenner & Ceci, 1994), which is shown again in Figure 5.1. It is included here because we now need to consider the material presented in the last four chapters against the societal environment in which children live and learn. Bronfenbrenner's model is a powerful guide in helping us understand human development and in supporting children's physical and mental wellness (Hamwey, Allen, Hay, & Varpio, 2019). The assessment of children's social and emotional wellness does not take place in a vacuum. It takes place in many nested environments – family, school, community, public health structures, mass media, as well as in economic and historical systems – to which children are exposed. Any final discussion of the assessment of children's social and emotional readiness and wellness for learning must consider the broader context

DOI: 10.4324/9781003152781-5

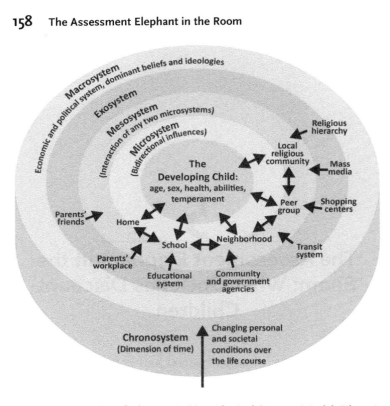

Figure 5.1 Urie Bronfenbrenner's Bioecological Systems Model. The microsystem impacts the child directly (e.g., parents, and teachers); The mesosystem includes interactions of microsystems such as how parents and teachers relate to each other; The exosystem contains larger institutions such as public health; The macrosystem involves cultural values such as how children are viewed and treated; and the chronosystem involves the historical context. Image by Ian Joslin is licensed under CC BY 4.0.

in which children are living. Any assessment of children will be influenced by the values and beliefs that the broader society holds. In the middle of a global pandemic and the corresponding response many governments and public health officials have imposed on schools, families and children, some might say that the context and outlook for students are grim.

The Systems in Which Children Find Themselves

History provides too many examples and reminders of the conditions in schools and families that can derail and compromise children's wellbeing. History also shows us that the values and beliefs that pervade society can disrupt children's welfare (Haring, Sorin, & Caltabiano, 2019). Haring et al. (2019) describe how changing conceptions of children over time ranging from denying their voice to recognizing their agency have increasingly influenced how well children can be protected from abuse and neglect. This is one of the reasons the United Nations Convention on the Rights of the Child (CRC, 1989) was developed and must be kept at the fore when considering any strategic educational action in the service of children's best interest.

Children arrive at school bearing the gifts and/or scars of the events they have encountered outside of school. Teachers must be open and culturally humble to recognize that what happens to children outside the classroom impacts learning in the classroom. Wars, violence, displacement, poverty, illness and power discrepancies between adults and children impact children in ways that teachers may not be aware of but nonetheless have a duty to learn about and understand. *This is one of the reasons why responsible teaching is demanding and difficult.* Educators must have the cultural humility to recognize what they do not know, what they think they know but need to verify and be open to seeking out information that allows proper practice for working and protecting children. Teachers are duty bearers.

However, not only teachers bear responsibility. Other adults can enact policies that profoundly help or harm the wellness of children. Thus, the *cultural humility* practices of teachers or any adult responsible for children's welfare should entail more than what Tervalon and Murray-Garcia (1998) describe as (a) a lifelong commitment to self-evaluation and self-critique, (b) the effort to rectify imbalances of power and (c) the inclusion of partnerships for advocacy. Cultural humility, as it specifically pertains to children, must also include recognition that a child's social and cultural context – its microsystem as shown in Figure 5.1 – can be severely disrupted by expert adults.

Expert adults in positions of power, such as teachers, politicians and medical doctors, may profess to act in children's best interest but not actually be doing so. The residential school system enacted to assimilate Indigenous people into Euro-Canadian society is a case in point (Brant, 2020). But we have others. Indeed, we have historical evidence of the disadvantaged position children generally occupy in society (Haring et al., 2019). We also have evidence that the slowness of recognizing children's needs can lead to a legacy of harm for children (Shaw & DeJong, 2012; Waechter et al., 2019). We need to do far better to protect children. Thus, cultural humility is necessary for all adults whose work can impact children's welfare.

It is for this reason that a book about the assessment of children's social and emotional readiness and wellbeing must include a chapter on how the COVID-19 pandemic *response* is impacting the social and emotional wellness of children. Historically, public health policy has been slow to recognize children's needs, for example, the physical abuse of children was once a case in point (Kempe, Silverman, Steele, Droegemueller, & Silver, 1962; Shaw & DeJong, 2012). Today we have a new domain of neglect and it revolves around children's welfare in the public health response to the pandemic. Although some health officials have sounded the alarm on children's needs during the COVID-19 pandemic (Thomas, Anurudran, Robb, & Burke, 2020), the public health *policy* of many nations during this time has not served children well. Public health policy resides in the exosystem of children's world (see Figure 5.1). It matters greatly to children's wellbeing. One cannot expect teachers to engage in doing what is in children's best interest in the classroom if other actors such as public health officials and government are effectively overlooking children's needs and even creating a systemic culture of harm. This is the elephant in the room, and that elephant cannot be ignored.

Sacrificing Children during the COVID-19 Pandemic Response

The writing of this book took place during a historic, tragic and ongoing natural experiment – the COVID-19 pandemic and the societal action in response. Starting in March 2020, schools, universities and many non-essential businesses closed in many parts of the United States, Canada and around the world as part of a desperate governmental response to curb the spread of the virus. Employees, where possible, were asked to work from home. Many teachers taught classes online using video platforms such as Google Meet, Zoom and others. Countless students were sent home to learn virtually. In the process, not only were typical curricular efforts upended but so were many social and emotional programs for children and youth (Morelli et al., 2020). In fact, a large study I was conducting on elementary school students' emotional responses to feedback was abruptly terminated. Parents and teachers came under enormous stress; not only from the immediate fear of the unknowns associated with the virus linked to COVID-19 but also the looming fear emerging from the uncertainty related to employment and child care. In their study of parental and children's socio-emotional functioning during the COVID-19 restrictions and lockdowns, Morelli et al. (2020) indicated the psychological risks that were emerging:

> **All these data highlight the importance of not underestimating the psychological risks that children and their families could face. In a report on May 13th, 2020, the United Nations also underlined how, during the COVID-19 pandemic, the emotional problems of children and adolescents were exacerbated by family stress, social isolation, interruption of school and educational activity, and uncertainty for the future which occurred in critical moments of their emotional development (United Nations, 2020).**
>
> **(Morelli et al. 2020, p. 2)**

Another perspective is that the COVID-19 pandemic has laid bare the priorities societies hold; these are the aspects of the environment that reside in the *macrosystem* of Bronfenbrenner's model. Societal values and beliefs about what children need, how they should be treated and protected reveal why children are and continue to be so vulnerable in the 21st century – even within first world countries that proclaim to value children as the most precious resource. If children were truly considered our most precious resource, we would not implement public health policies that exacerbate educational, social and emotional declines in children during a pandemic that most seriously targets older adults (Morelli et al., 2020; United Nations, 2020). Public health strategies must be balanced to protect the vulnerable; but vulnerability is not just physical, it is also psychological. When it really matters, as in the throes of a health crisis, we would expect that the most powerful and learned members of our society would implement the most balanced and least harmful approaches to protect members of the population. As a segment of the population, children are vulnerable because they are small, powerless and rely on adults to act on their behalf. Although children are one of the most resilient groups to avoid hospitalization and survive COVID-19, many would claim that they have been dealt the worst hand in this pandemic.

The Children Are Not Alright: What the Data Reveal

When the public health pandemic responses rolled out in my hometown, Edmonton, Alberta, my growing concern was not about the virus. Instead, I grew concerned about the perilous situation for many K-12 students who were forced to stay home, in some cases in highly adverse home conditions. Many children were not only missing out on their education since much of the virtual learning was ill-planned but also were deprived from access to safe outlets for social interaction – much of which is found at school. Several news sources reported on increased domestic violence and child abuse; the rise was also reported in academic papers (Bucerius, Roberts, & Jones, 2021). Speaking to our University newspaper, FOLIO, I was asked: what keeps you up at night? I responded that what I was especially concerned about was the social isolation of teenagers. But I was also thinking about children generally (McMaster, 2020). As a psychologist I am aware that home is not a safe space for many children; and now many children were having to face being in a confined space 24/7 with stressed parents who themselves felt besieged and without much recourse. This was a recipe for disaster.

Conducting a webinar for the University's External Relations on Helping Your Children Get Through the COVID-19 lockdown (Leighton, 2020), I saw first-hand the desperation of many parents who joined me during the presentation. Child advocacy organizations sounded the alarm but, truthfully, many of these organizations have done little to help children. Some of these supposed child advocacy organizations have, in fact, justified the punitive public health measures put in place, which have worked against children. Without calling out any specific organization, one of the lessons for me of this pandemic is that child advocacy groups have revealed themselves to be more partisan in their political affiliations than one would have assumed, perhaps naively. Some advocacy organizations are not really in the business of serving children's best interests.

The pandemic response has harmed children in several ways. Can we generate casual inferences from the accumulated data and studies? Not very well. It would be unethical to conduct randomized control studies of how school closures, social distancing and masking might cause a decline in children's social and emotional, and even academic wellness. Nonetheless, as with so much of the evidence collected during this pandemic, there is a growing and powerful correlational (circumstantial) case to show that the public health response has harmed and continues to harm many children. The one-size-fits-all response of many governments has injured those children who are the least able to afford missing school and who have the most to gain from being at school, engaging in interactions with teachers and other children and participating in social and emotional programs. In other words, the most vulnerable children are actively hurt by expert adults who have the power to do better; duty bearers who have abdicated their responsibility to children.

Many reports now reveal that children's academic performance and mental health have decreased significantly during the pandemic response while physical unwellness – childhood obesity – has increased (e.g., Cost et al., 2021; Deoni, Beauchemin, Volpe, D'Sa, & the RESONANCE Consortium, 2021). A recent study by Deoni and colleagues (2021) at Brown University revealed that babies born in Rhode Island during the pandemic showed a drop of 22 points on the Mullen Scales of early learning compared to the average of prior cohorts. The Mullen Scales provide a measure of cognitive development akin to an Intelligence Quotient (IQ) score (Mullen, 1995; Staples, MacDonald, & Zimmer, 2012). The size of this drop was reported to be similar to what has been observed with institutionalized orphans. Deoni et al. (2021) attributed the drop in performance to the lockdown and social isolation restrictions imposed on participating families rather than on the virus associated with COVID-19. Participating mothers and babies were screened for the virus prior to inclusion in the study, and none had contracted the virus. Likewise, in Montgomery County, Bethesda, literacy performance for 2nd, 5th, 8th and 11th grade students declined by 35.3, 23.5, 10.8 and 9.2 percentage points, respectively, in comparison to performance before schools were closed for the pandemic (Peetz, 2021). Also, for math performance, the drop for these same four grades was 20.6, 25.8, 14.2 and 2.3 percentage points, respectively, in comparison to performance prior to the shuttering of schools. The youngest students declined the most, as did Black, Hispanic and limited English proficiency students by the move from in person to virtual learning. In the province of Alberta, school closures and the shift to online learning also disadvantaged the most vulnerable young readers in the development of reading skills (Betkowski, 2020).

In a cross-sectional study of almost 1,500 children and youth published in the *European Child and Adolescent Psychiatry* journal, Cost et al. (2021) reported that 67–70% of children and adolescents experienced a decline in mental health during the first wave of the COVID-19 response. Although the rate of decline was greater in children between the ages of 6 and 18 years (70.2%) compared to children between two and five years (66.1%), most children experienced a worsening of depression, anxiety and irritability. Cost and colleagues attributed the decline to social isolation, loss of in person social interactions and difficulty in complying with restrictions. These results and conclusions are comparable to other studies in China (Zhou et al., 2020), Germany (Ravens-Sieberer et al., 2021), Canada (Gadermann et al., 2020), Brazil (Garcia de Avila et al., 2020), India (Saurabh & Ranjan, 2020), Italy (Spinelli, Lionetti, Pastore, & Fasolo, 2020) and Spain (Ezpeleta, Navarro, de la Osa,

Trepat, & Penelo, 2020). Moreover, in a review of the effects of pandemic responses on children's obesity, Browne et al. (2021) indicated that the pandemic response, which has led to increased sedentary behaviors from stay-at-home orders, closing of gyms and physical distancing had led to an:

> increased risk [for children] to develop obesity and [has exacerbated] obesity disease severity. The once familiar environments of family, home, school, and community and their multi-factorial interactions have changed to unrecognizable scenarios, increasing stress for children and families. The impact of stress on both diseases, characterized by inflammation and weakened immune response and exacerbated by disparities, affects health, economic, and social outcomes.
>
> (p. 96)

One could comprehend severe response measures in light of the COVID-19 risk if there were evidence that these responses increased student safety and reduced spread of the virus. However, approximately 18 months after schools shuttered across many parts of the world, it has become increasingly evident from the data that schools are not places of excess infection or spread (Willyard, 2021). For example, in one of the largest studies examining the spread of the virus associated with COVID-19, North Carolina researchers surveyed an excess of 90,000 students (Zimmerman et al., 2021). The researchers found that rates of virus transmission were lower for children in school than outside of school (Zimmerman et al., 2021). The journal *Nature*, one of the most respected scientific journals, published the news feature of the comparative results as shown in Figure 5.2 (Willyard, 2021). What these results, based on high-quality data, show are that schools are not places of virulent spread.

The Responsibility to Understand Data to Protect Children

My field of study is not epidemiology, immunology, or public health, it is psychology and children's development and learning. Many research and experimental psychologists are trained

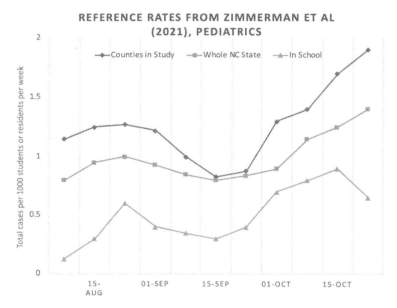

Figure 5.2 Author created graph showing the relative cases of COVID-19 per 1,000 people in three distinct domains. Graph is based on numbers provided in Zimmerman et al. (2021). Incidence and secondary transmission of SARS-CoV-2 infections in schools. Pediatrics, 147(4).

in data science and research methods. We understand the difference between correlation, causation, the value of randomized control trials and representative samples. I say this to underscore the fact that many psychologists can make sense of public health data and can detect the lack of evidence for certain conclusions and decisions that have been made in light of the desire to stop the spread of a virus. One does not have to be an epidemiologist to evaluate conclusions in light of the study designs and data that undergird those conclusions. Although it is beyond the scope of this chapter to engage in a specific discussion of the political aspect of the decisions to close schools, mask children and in some cases even recommend inoculation against COVID-19 for children, it is my opinion that children have not been served well in Canada and in many parts of the United

States. As previously mentioned, children are being harmed by the responses that many politicians and public health officials decided to enact in the name of public safety.

The response to the COVID-19 pandemic has become politicized. Open discussion of risk, costs, benefits and the scientific evidence underlying public health measures was curtailed if not outright dismissed several months after the start of the pandemic as I illustrate later in this chapter. This matters to any discussion of social and emotional assessment in schools in 2021 and beyond. Schools reside within a broader environment, including a scientific community, and if this broader environment is 'poisoning the well' for children, the poison will undoubtedly affect what is discussed, suppressed and even done in the classroom. In the next section, I document the ways public health has failed children and by implication also failed educators and parents who wish to protect children's readiness and wellbeing for learning.

Children's Rights When It Matters: A Series of Failures

There are many organizations that claim to support and advocate for children. Some of them, such as the Canadian Pediatric Society (www.cps.ca), Children First Canada (childrenfirstcanada. org), the American Academy of Pediatrics (www.aap.org) and the Centers for Disease Control and Prevention (CDC) (www. cdc.gov), often do outstanding work. These organizations have brought attention to many physical and mental health issues with which children struggle, and have created useful resources for educators, parents and psychologists alike. In addition, some of these organizations have provided political leadership. For example, Children First Canada, as a charitable organization, lobbies and petitions the Federal Government for policy support related to children's injuries, mental health, discrimination, child abuse, diseases, poverty, food insecurity, bullying and physical activity. Children First Canada even organizes young Canadians to get involved in government. I have used many of their resources during my university instruction of pre-service teachers.

Prior to the COVID-19 health crisis, organizations such as these had not had the opportunity to advocate for children during a global pandemic. However, in the past 18 months, observations of their advocacy are made possible. To be fair, this is not an easy time to advocate for children given the volatility of the situation, the complexity of the medical evidence, and the stigma associated with speaking out against public health policy; also, the psychological impacts of the pandemic response on children are just beginning to take form. Nonetheless, given wide-spread actions such as school lockdowns, transfers of in-person instruction to virtual learning, masking of children upon return to in-person instruction and/or social isolation due to enhanced safety precautions, the time is ripe to observe the beginnings of advocacy.

Surprisingly, *actionable* advocacy for children's best interests during the COVID-19 pandemic has been absent from many of these organizations. Organizations such as the Canadian Pediatric Society, Children First Canada and the American Academy of Pediatrics, have not challenged interpretations of data, which show that children are the *least vulnerable* to the harmful effects of the virus. Consider that children as a group are at an extremely low risk of showing adverse symptoms, hospitalization and death (Government of Canada, 2021). For example, of the 316,803 children in Canada who tested positive for COVID-19 as of September 24, 2021, only 2% or 1,671 were hospitalized in *all* of Canada. Of the 1,671 children hospitalized, only 1.2% or 191 were admitted into an Intensive Care Unit (ICU). Of those in ICU, .01% or 16 died. Any death is tragic. But this is also when data-driven and judicious leadership from health experts and governments was needed to responsibly assess relative risks and harms. Therefore, the fact that many schools stayed closed or threatened to close if a child tested positive for the virus was unconscionable, especially once teachers became able to be vaccinated if they did not already have natural immunity.

Child advocacy organizations have not vociferously advocated for schools to stay open, teachers to be vaccinated and children to be unmasked. Instead, many of these organizations have bowed to political and public health pressure and the accompanying narrative of a single response to ensure public safety. The position statements from many of these organizations do not reflect decades of accepted knowledge about what is needed to maintain children's social and emotional wellness. For example, Children First Canada, in a statement released on July 30, 2021 criticized the chief medical officer of the province of Alberta for lifting many restrictions on children's schooling. This was a rare move on the part of the province in heeding the data in light of children's negligible risk. Instead, according to Children First Canada, the provincial health order "placed children and youth at very grave risk" (Children First Canada, 2021). In fact, there were no data offered from Children First Canada to suggest that children and youth were being placed in grave risk. Observing some of the Twitter messages of the CEO of Children First Canada, one observes messages that fail to properly represent children's risks with the backing of data. For example, Figure 5.3 shows that there is a tweet claiming "exponential growth" in children's COVID-19 cases in Alberta. At the time of this tweet, however, the reproduction number of the spread did not show exponential growth in major cities.

Although published local news reports revealed that children between the ages of five and nine years of age had the most active infections at 724.9 per 100,000 people (CTV, 2021), there was no evidence that active infections were increasing at an exponential rate. Indeed, hospitalizations for children were the lowest of any age group as shown in Figure 5.4.

Based on such observations, it is difficult to avoid the question of what motivates powerful and expert adults, claiming to be child advocates, in sharing incorrect information about children's risk. On the one hand, it is possible the CEO lacks simple data literacy; misunderstandings of data plagues many who might be working on behalf of children given that it requires statistical reasoning, which is not a widely taught skill. On the other hand, it is possible that some of these organizations have political interests and motives. Questioning an unpopular government's chief medical officer may be part of an overall strategic plan to undermine their leadership.

Comparative data must be considered in actionable advocacy for children's social and emotional wellness. Currently, the data show that children are at a surprisingly low risk of adverse outcomes from COVID-19 to warrant the harm being inflicted

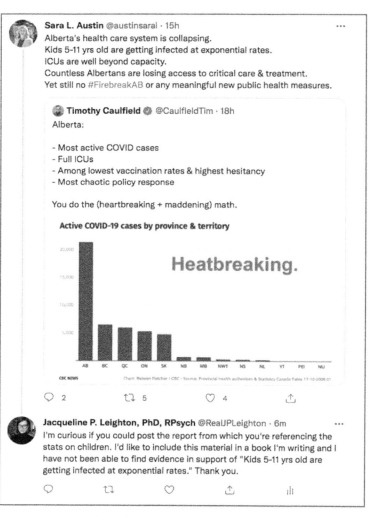

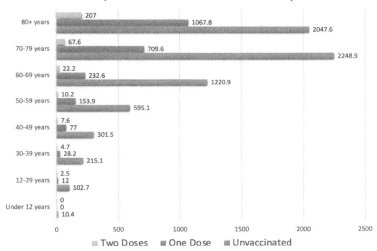

COVID-19 in Alberta: Hospitalizations by Status in Vaccination Rate per 100K measured across the last 120 days

Figure 5.4 Author generated graph based on COVID-19 in Alberta on Sept 28th, 2021. R values are updated every 2 weeks by Alberta Health. No R values are reported for children separately. Latest R values for Alberta (provincewide) reported on Sept 28, 2021 were less than 1 for two largest cities in Alberta – Edmonton (0.97) and Calgary (0.94). According to Kohlberg and Neyman (2020), if R > 1 then daily new infection "explode" exponentially. If R < 1 then daily new infection decays to zero (p. 6).

on them in the name of public safety. Compared to injuries and deaths from drowning, vehicular accidents, flu and cancer among children 1–4 years, COVID-19 poses almost no threat (Leonhardt, 2021). For example, annual deaths among children 1–4 years from vehicle accidents is 2.3 per 100,000 versus 0.2 per 100,000 from COVID-19. Likewise, deaths among children 5–14 years from vehicle accidents is 1.9 per 100,000 versus 0.2 per 100,000 from COVID-19. Thus, depending on the political narratives of countries, provinces and states, jurisdictions have selectively interpreted data and taken on different health policies. To be sure, some jurisdictions have kept schools open; others have closed with virtual learning. Some schools require students to mask indoors and/or outdoors. Other schools do not require masks at all. For example, unlike New York, Florida has had very few restrictions on individuals, schools and children. Unlike Australia, Canada and the United States, Sweden has had very few restrictions as well. Although comparing different jurisdictions is fraught with problems due to differences not only in particular health strategies, but also on myriad other factors such as wealth, geographical location, infrastructure and compliance, one thing is indisputable: Health has become highly political and children are part of the political machinations.

The First Failure of Public Health in Protecting Children's Wellness

The first failure has been choking off debate about data. Diverse, strategic questioning of data is necessary for protecting children's present and future. The blocking of debate about data has been observed in the silencing of highly respected medical professionals who have offered different ideas for dealing with the pandemic. For example, on November 24, 2020, *the Lancet,* a prominent medical journal featured a post on herd immunity in relation to COVID-19. The article highlighted how three highly respected epidemiologists from Stanford University (Dr. Jay Bhattacharya), Oxford University (Dr. Suneptra Gupta) and Harvard University (Dr. Martin Kulldorff) offered a different approach to combat the COVID-19 pandemic. Called the *Great Barrington Declaration* and endorsed by thousands of medical practitioners, Bhattacharya, Gupta and Kulldorff (2020) wrote about focused protection:

> **Coming from both the left and right, and around the world, we have devoted our careers to protecting people. Current lockdown policies are producing devastating effects on short and long-term public health. The results (to name a few) include lower childhood vaccination rates, worsening cardiovascular disease outcomes, fewer cancer screenings and deteriorating mental health — leading to greater excess mortality in years to come, with the working class and younger members of society carrying the heaviest burden. Keeping students out of school is a grave injustice.**

(n.p.n)

The Declaration was challenged in weeks by another group of experts. The challenge came in the form of the *John Snow memorandum*, which was written to defend the massive restrictions that were being imposed, including indiscriminate lockdowns and masking on most of the population (Burki, 2020). The John Snow memorandum also had thousands of supporters and described the *focused protection* articulated in the Declaration as a "dangerous fallacy." However, relative risk and focused protection are not fallacies; such concepts are considered in almost every aspect of modern health policy. Indeed, the Declaration was not the product of a fringe group; it was advanced by some of our most respected medical experts.

The focused protection advanced by the Barrington Declaration was undeniably more attuned to children's rights and their social and emotional health than the approach offered by supporters of the John Snow memorandum. Focused protection considers the concept of risk in how individuals are helped and this is especially relevant in how children are treated. Bhattacharya et al. (2020) wrote:

> **The aim of focused protection is to minimize overall mortality from both COVID-19 and other diseases by balancing the need to protect high-risk individuals from COVID-19 while reducing the harm that lockdowns have had on other aspects of medical care and public health. It recognizes that public health is concerned with the health and well-being of populations in a broader way than just infection control.**
>
> **(para. 3)**

High-risk individuals are those who are of an advanced age and who have several comorbidities, with obesity being one of the most lethal for surviving COVID-19 (Mahase, 2020).

Unfortunately for children, the John Snow memorandum (Alwan et al., 2020) gained support and led to the marginalization of the medical experts associated with the Barrington Declaration. Suddenly, the narrative about how to best deal with COVID-19 became a monologue about correct and incorrect approaches to public health. In fact, questioning the restrictions and tactics used by public health officials in positions of power (e.g., Anthony Fauci in the United States and Teresa Tam in

Figure 5.5 A Screenshot of a Tweet Showing the Professional Bullying Taking Place Among Medical Scientists.

Canada) was soon considered to be methods of *misinformation.* A tweet from Martin Kulldorff, shown in Figure 5.5, one of the co-authors of the Barrington Declaration reveals how his co-author, Jay Bhattacharya, even became the subject of a smear campaign by colleagues at Stanford University (Heneghan & Kulldorff, 2021). The audacity to question current COVID-19 guidelines such as the efficacy of cloth masks was now considered to be outright propaganda.

Following the "science" has thus become less about thinking critically and more about blindly accepting a single narrative about how best to handle the pandemic. *This was the first failure of public health for protecting children* – the dismissal of perspectives such as focused protection, which actively considered children's health and wellness.

The Second Failure of Public Health in Protecting Children's Wellness

The second failure stems from the first failure. By choking off a debate about data, children's overall health has been actively harmed. The gross neglect of children's welfare during the COVID-19 pandemic response will undoubtedly be recorded as yet another human rights injustice perpetrated against the most vulnerable amongst us. We are living through another time period of atrociously poor judgment in the Western world. In Canada, we have lived through others such as the creation and maintenance of residential schools (Marshall & Gallant, 2021) and the practice of eugenics between the 1930s and 1970s (Marshall & Robertson, 2019; also Stern, 2005). It is remarkable how human rights abuses are often defended as they occur on the basis of the "public good." Recall that the justification for residential schools was advanced by respected government and church officials as suitable courses of action in the best interest of society. Likewise, many respected officials, including doctors, supported the case for the forced sterilization of women:

> Many prominent Canadians of that era were advocates of eugenics philosophy and eugenic sterilization, including Dr. E.W. McBride, Professor Carrie Derick and Dr. Helen MacMurchy. Support for eugenic sterilization was also expressed in the 1920s by many prominent Alberta women, including Emily Murphy and Nellie McClung. Maternal feminists like McClung, for example, argued that women were the mothers and guardians of their "race."
>
> (Marshall & Roberston, 2019, para. 6)

In human rights abuses, the veil of public good is indeed often used as a rationale. Consider the account of the experimentation done on Indigenous children (MacDonald, Stanwisk, & Lynk, 2014). MacDonald et al. (2014) detail "highly unethical experiments" by respected doctors and government officials in the name of science:

> The experiments were performed by the Department of Indian Affairs of Canada under the direction of two physicians: Dr Percy Moore, the Indian Affairs Branch Superintendent of Medical Services, and Dr Frederick Tisdall, a famed nutritionist, a former president of the Canadian Paediatric Society and one of three paediatricians at The Hospital for Sick Children (Toronto, Ontario) who developed Pablum infant cereal in the 1930s. In these experiments, parents were not

informed, nor were consents obtained. Even as children died, the experiments continued. Even after the recommendations from the Nuremberg trial, these experiments continued.

(n.p.n)

It has often been said that a society shows its collective moral compass by the treatment of its most vulnerable citizens. This pandemic has laid bare what public health, government and large segments of society think and feel about children. The fact that most countries, states, provinces and jurisdictions have chosen to impose public health measures that hurt school-age children does not bode well for societies that aim to measure and sustain children's social and emotional wellness.

Why Closing Schools and Masking Hurts Children

It is understandable that early on in the pandemic, many schools in Canada, the United States and other countries closed for in person learning and, instead, went fully remote (Aurini & Davies, 2021). Sweden was an exception (Vlachos, Hertegård, & Svaleryd, 2021). However, by the time vaccines were made available, the justification to continue with school closures and masking became less clear. Schools not only provide a structured environment for children to engage in academic activities, schools also provide the hands-on materials for doing much of the academic work required. For example, Frenette, Frank and Deng (2020) showed that over 4.25% of children in the lowest income quartile had no internet with which to engage in virtual learning. Moreover, Greenlee and Reid (2020) reported that only 67% of children with parents having less than a high school education participated in structured academic activities three times a week. For children with parents with a bachelor's degree or higher, 80% of children engaged in such activities.

In a crowdsourcing study of participants' concern due to the COVID-19 pandemic for their children aged 0–14 years, Arim, Findlay and Kohen (2020) found that children with disabilities were worse off than children without disabilities. In every category of concern, a greater percentage of participants were more concerned about their children with disabilities than those without disabilities – for example, general physical health (27.6 vs 21.6), mental health (60.4 vs 42.8), loneliness or isolation (63.0 vs 51.6), academic success (57.6 vs 35.6), opportunities to socialize with friends (73.8 vs 70.2), amount of screen time (72.6 vs 61.7), online safety (34.4 vs 22.3), amount of physical activity (49.4 vs 35.5) and eating junk food and sweets (28.3 vs 20.0). Indeed, compared to pre-pandemic levels, youth aged 15 to 24 were found to show the greatest level of worsened mental health relative to all other age categories (Statistics Canada, 2020).

The overall picture that emerges from the unfocused protection taken by public health officials in Canada and the United States as examples is one of sacrificing the young for the protection of the old. During teachers' vaccine uptake, many children have been forced to wear masks during in-class instruction, and to maintain safe distances from each other. At the start of September 2021, children heading back to school in Alberta and Ontario were required to wear masks during the day. Prior to the start of the school year, Public Health Ontario (2021) released a memo stating the following:

> **There [are] limited studies directly evaluating the isolated effectiveness of mask wearing in children. However, several studies found that mask mandates in schools have been associated with lower incidence of severe acute respiratory coronavirus 2 (SARS-CoV-2) infection. Wearing masks for outdoor sporting events is unlikely to be beneficial.**
>
> **(p. 1)**

The problem with the six indoor masking studies cited in this memo is that all are correlational. Not a single study employed randomized control trials. This means that any causal inference about mask wearing and reduced transmission is unsubstantiated. Reduced transmission may have little to do with masks and more to do with lower levels of speaking amongst children and activity levels generally. Although Public Health Ontario does not state that mask mandates *cause* lower transmission and is clear to state that masks in schools have only been *associated*

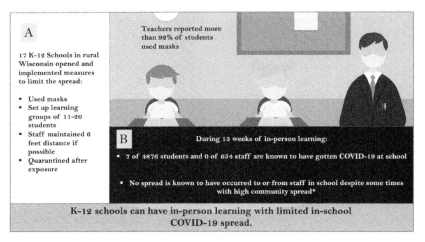

Figure 5.6 Author created graphic based on the graphic used in Falk et al. (2021), which includes unsubstantiated causal insinuations for masking children. Panel A include observed variables, but they are not causal. Panel B includes outcome variables but there is no causal link established with Panel A. *No cause-and-effect inference is possible because students were not randomly assigned to different masking groups and compared to a control. All the relationships described are correlational without controlling the effects of third variables.

with a lower incidence of infection, the recklessness is that most of their readers would not know the difference. Thus, the memo tacitly supports the illusion that there is strong scientific evidence for masking, and therefore that masking children is warranted. By referencing studies like Falk et al. (2021), one of the six indoor masking studies included in the memo, Public Health Ontario risks misleading parents and educators about the strength of the scientific evidence undergirding their recommendations. For example, Figure 5.6 shows a pictograph similar in information to the one found in Falk et al. (2021). The pictograph is designed to convey reassuring information to parents and educators about specific precautions and outcomes, but evidence for causal links among variables does not exist.

None of the observed variables shown in Panel A of Figure 5.6 have been shown to be causally related to the outcome variables shown in Panel B. Indeed, this type of graphic is ripe for misinterpretation by teachers and parents, who may have little knowledge that *correlation does not signify causation*, or that quality of research design matters in judging the merit of study results. Another problem with the six studies cited by Public Health Ontario is that none of these studies were subject to the typical peer review process (Dawson et al., 2021; Falk et al., 2021). The studies were part of the CDC's *Morbidity and Mortality Weekly Report* and not associated with independent scientific journals.

Randomized controlled trials are needed to causally evaluate the efficacy of masks and other non-pharmaceutical interventions (NPIs) for mandating strong public health recommendations.

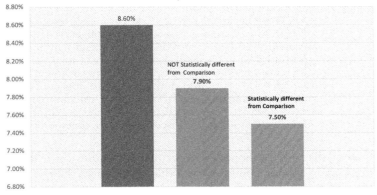

Figure 5.7 Author designed graph of the reduction in symptoms aggregated across age groups based on type of mask worn (cloth vs surgical) compared to no mask worn in Comparison villages. Cloth masks did not lead to a statistically significant reduction in symptoms (8.5% relative reduction, p=.048); Surgical masks did lead to a statistically significant reduction in symptoms (13.6 relative reduction, p=.000). Results from Abaluck, J., Kwong, L.H., Styczynski et al. (2021). The impact of community masking on COVID-19: A cluster-randomized trial in Bangladesh. Discussion Papers. 1086. https://elischolar.library.yale.edu/egcenter-discussion-paper-series/1086.

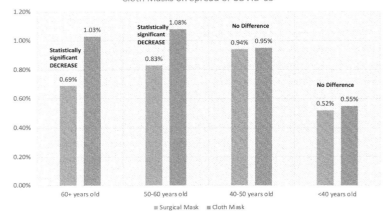

Figure 5.8 Author designed graph of the difference in spread of COVID-19 between type of mask worn (cloth vs surgical) disaggregated across age groups. Surgical masks lead to a statistically significant reduction in spread only for age groups 50-60 years (p=.011) and 60+ year (p=.001). No difference for other age groups. Results from Abaluck, J., Kwong, L.H., Styczynski et al. (2021). The impact of community masking on COVID-19: A cluster-randomized trial in Bangladesh. Discussion Papers. 1086. https://elischolar. library.yale.edu/egcenter-discussion-paper-series/1086.

One of the only randomized experimental studies on real-life masking by human beings showed that cloth masks did not lead to a statistically significant reduction in virus transmission. As shown in Figures 5.7 and 5.8, cloth masks did not significantly reduce transmission compared to the control condition of no masking, but surgical masks did significantly help reduce transmission compared to the control. However, when the researchers looked more closely at the effects of surgical masks by age group (see Figure 5.8), they found that surgical masks only helped reduce transmission compared to the control for adults older than 50 years (Abaluck et al., 2021).

Given the dearth of causal evidence on real-life masking, it is necessary to ponder why public health officials would recommend that children wear non-medical or cloth masks during the school day. In fact, the benefits of masking children are doubtful given the overall lack of evidence for cloth masks to prevent transmission of airborne viruses. Public Ontario Health acknowledged that very few studies had been conducted on the *psychological consequences* of mask use in children. However, we do have a body of related theoretical and biological arguments that should dissuade us from masking students as masking can interfere with children's social interactions, language expression and non-verbal communication.

Prior to COVID-19, the essentiality of reading faces was an accepted and standard part of our bioecological understanding of healthy human development. Babies observe and read faces and this aids in the development of their brain circuitry (Lopatina, Komleva, Gorina, Higashida, & Salmina, 2018; Tierney & Nelson, 2009; Yogman et al., 2018). Babies and young children who are in the early phases of forming attachments to parents depend on parental facial expressions as part of a collective set of communicative cues that help them establish emotional bonds with significant adults (Winston & Chicot, 2016). Teachers also serve as secondary attachment figures (see Chapters 1 and 2 in this volume); thus, we can speculate that seeing teachers' faces is also helpful to children (Pianta, 2016). Using magnetic brain imaging, Sethna et al. (2017) demonstrated that barriers to mother-infant interactions can be a source of stress for babies, and negatively influence brain connectivity and growth. The importance of facial processing is hardly surprising given that human beings are born with predispositions to process facial attributes (Green, Staff, Bromley, Jones, & Petty, 2021):

> [Inborn predispositions] are thought to be already present at birth and essential for face processing to occur. The complex face-perception system in an infant becomes focused and refined as the result of a combination of evolutionary inheritance and experience-dependent exposures, thought to be associated with neural pruning of under-stimulated synaptic connections and neural strengthening of those that are regularly exposed to stimuli.
>
> (Scott, Pascalis, & Nelson, 2007; Simion & Giorgio, 2015, p. 23)

In discussing the benefits and burdens of face masks among school children, Spitzer (2020), a psychiatrist, considers the interference they pose in hospital settings:

> **Of particular relevance for schools may be the experiences with face masks in hospitals, including psychiatric hospitals, such as the clinic which I am heading. I implemented the general use of face masks for all staff and patients on March 16th 2020, and it soon became clear that they interfere with practicing psychiatry: The decreased emotional observability made the job harder to do. A psychotherapist wrote me an email, noting that socially complicated and challenging inpatients in psychotherapy are very difficult to treat, "as dissociative states and tensions are much harder to detect early enough so that appropriate interventions can be performed. In addition, exposition training (such as in patients after trauma, patients with panic disorder, and patients with obsessive compulsive disorder, OCD) which implies the conscious provocation of anxiety, are hard to do with a face mask obstructing the perception of the patient's emotions. [...] Even in diagnostic interviews, face masks interfere with decisions regarding diagnosis and therapy"**
>
> **(Bosch, personal communication [11])**
>
> Spitzer, 2020, p. 6)

In a recent Intelligencer article for *New York Magazine*, Zweig (2021) reported that many nations, including the United Kingdom, Ireland, Scandinavia, France, the Netherlands, Switzerland and Italy, excuse students of varying ages from masking. Canada and most states in the United States, surprisingly, have shown an absence of evidence-based action in support of children. Most US states, with the exception of 22, claim to be fully open and yet continue to enforce young children to wear masks in public buildings (Bunis & Rough, 2021). Indeed, the stricter guidance from the CDC for masking children is at odds with guidance even from the World Health Organization. Although data are more difficult to track in Canada, as this is being written most provinces require students to wear masks in public buildings.

The masking of children in Canada and the United States highlights how public health policy, in the absence of strong scientific evidence, can negatively affect the lives of children. There is no conclusive evidence that cloth masks reduce the spread of the virus; masks may even increase the spread (see MacIntyre et al., 2015). Moreover, children are at an incredibly low risk of presenting with poor outcomes if they do become infected. In fact, the World Health Organization (2020) published guidelines recognizing that policies on masks should prioritize the child. This advice has not been heeded in many parts of the United States and Canada. Although some might argue that masking students is less harmful than closing schools, the issue is that neither may have been necessary to protect children in a focused manner as some marginalized medical experts recommended early on and still recommend. The weight of the evidence clearly indicates that children are at very low risk of poor outcomes from disease. Moreover, teachers can be vaccinated. Thus, the continued implementation of masking children, imposing social distancing and even in some cases closing schools to reduce spread is not consistent with the available evidence, and, importantly, carry a significant risk to children's development. Within the exosystem of a child's overall environment, these actions are promoted in the service of 'public safety' with little regard for how children's social and emotional wellness is harmed.

Conclusion to the Book

A book about the assessment of children's social and emotional readiness and wellbeing must include mention of the societal values and beliefs that affect children. Schools and teachers do not operate in isolation. If the broader society is showing clear signs of struggle and offering quarrels amongst medical experts about how crises should be handled, the pandemonium will undoubtedly affect children, their families and practices at school. Throughout this book, I have maintained that a children's rights perspective is necessary to do what is in children's best interest. This perspective can be applied specifically to the administration of assessments to evaluate children's social and emotional readiness and wellbeing in schools. However, it would be a mistake to think that this perspective does not also apply to the larger society in which children live.

The meaning of social and emotional wellness with which I began this book was the following:

> Social and emotional readiness and wellbeing consists of two inter-related processes. The first process is social and involves being part of a group of learners that collaborates for the purpose of achieving learning goals. This process requires students to acquire ways of behaving that allow them to advance their own learning without hindering the learning of others. The second process is emotional and involves developing a sense of awareness about how to use affect – both negative and positive – constructively to achieve desired learning goals. The operationalization of these processes depends on the specific situation and students of interest.

When we consider the meaning of social and emotional wellness outlined here, it reads to be fairly localized in the classroom. But, we need to recognize that this meaning is fully dependent on what is happening broadly in society as well. Once upon a time, this broader view could have been comfortably avoided in first world countries like Canada and the United States. In first world countries, we used to think, large-scale disasters occur but they are properly addressed and typically short-lived. The wealth of infrastructure and knowledge that exists in such nations confers protection from almost any assault. This may not be true anymore. What we have observed during the COVID-19 pandemic is a societal response that has effectively silenced important expert opinion in consideration of all data and debate.

Debate may not be warranted at the start of an emergency where quelling the loss of life is the instinct. But if the emergency persists, and responses fail, then debate is not only warranted but essential to protect the most vulnerable. If a city is steeped in war, famine, or any other calamity for too long, children will be impacted, possibly without redress. Any service that existed prior to the disruption will likely be suspended, and children will likely be too afraid for their lives at home and in the classroom if they are lucky enough to still attend school.

It would be naïve to think that children's social and emotional wellness can be edified with a school program and sound assessments without taking into account the other environmental systems that envelope the child. Far from antiquated, this is precisely the hierarchy of needs Maslow specified in 1943 in the now famous paper on *A Theory of Human Motivation*. Without the basic needs met *outside* the classroom, and without a lifeline to stem the suffering, little else matters for the child *inside* the classroom. And so, in this era of a pandemic that has lasted over a year and may well last much longer, we need to consider the harm it has had on children, and how teachers and parents can begin to enact the three principles introduced in Chapter 1. The three principles again are:

> **PRINCIPLE 1. There is little cognitive learning for children without social and emotional readiness and wellbeing. Some children need help acquiring the social and emotional competencies, attributes, and/or skills that will help them achieve a state of social and emotional readiness and wellbeing for learning.**
>
> **PRINCIPLE 2. Social and emotional readiness and wellbeing can be formally or informally measured to yield data and inform interpretations about what is in the best interest of students, as rights holders, in their learning. These data can also be used to facilitate children's acquisition of social and emotional competencies, attributes and/or skills in classrooms.**
>
> **PRINCIPLE 3. Facilitating children's acquisition of social and emotional competencies, attributes and/or skills in the classroom requires earning children's trust. Trust comes about when teachers recognize and nurture their role as secondary attachment figures and as duty bearers in the lives of children.**

These principles hold relevance for children's learning. But these principles require adults to pay attention and enact them in the best interest of children's social and emotional health. Given what we have observed during the response to the COVID-19 crisis, it may be necessary to add a caveat to the three principles. The caveat must call attention to situations where the negligence of adults interferes with the actualization of these three principles in the classroom and results in harm to children.

Today, we are observing, in real-time, the implementation of health strategies on children and their families that not only conflict with these three principles but also decades of data about what we know to be in children's best interest and wellbeing. Any health directive that closes schools, classrooms, calls for social distancing, masking of children or virtual learning to mitigate a disease that hurts fewer children than automobile accidents, and can be rectified with adults being vaccinated, will undoubtedly come to be known as a human rights violation of children.

A painful lesson from the last two years is that greater responsibility is required from duty bearers outside the classroom; the ones who reside in the ecosystem and macrosystem (Bronfenbrenner & Ceci, 1994). Our first-world privileges have allowed us to effectively disregard these public actors with outsized responsibilities in children's lives. In nations where little goes wrong, parents, teachers and others have the luxury to become complacent about how political systems will treat children. However, we are no longer at this stage. When we observe government policy makers and public health officials enact policies that harm children and their families, there is not much teachers or psychologists can do to rectify the situation. However, we can learn from such events. We can speak out. We must continue to bring evidence to light because the consequences matter. When a school is forced to shutter, there is no social and emotional program and assessment plan that will be administered to a child. For the sake of children's rights, their wellbeing and learning, then, we need much greater account of the duty bearers that reside in the outer circles of children's lives. Maybe a caveat is not enough. Maybe a fourth principle needs to be added to the three we considered at the start of this book: *Before considering any social and emotional program or assessment, beware of the values and beliefs held in the larger society about children. Regardless of the rhetoric conveyed about children in social circles, if there is no political action behind the protection of children's rights, beware that anything implemented in the classroom can be disbanded; children's interests can be disregarded out of expediency despite scientific evidence to the contrary.*

Summary of Five Key Points

- Societal values and beliefs about what children need, how they should be treated and protected reveal why children are and continue to be so vulnerable in the 21st century – even within first world countries that proclaim to value children as the most precious resource. If children were truly considered our most precious resource, we would not implement public health policies that exacerbate educational, social and emotional declines in children during a pandemic that most seriously targets older adults (Morelli et al., 2020; United Nations, 2020).

- Many reports now reveal that children's academic performance and mental health have decreased significantly during the pandemic response while physical unwellness – childhood obesity – has increased (e.g., Cost et al., 2021; Deoni, Beauchemin, Volpe, D'Sa, & the RESONANCE Consortium, 2021).
- Surprisingly, *actionable* advocacy for children's best interests during the COVID-19 pandemic has been absent from many of these organizations. Organizations such as the Canadian Pediatric Society, Children First Canada and the American Academy of Pediatrics, have not challenged interpretations of data, which show that children are the *least vulnerable* to the harmful effects of the virus.
- Following the 'science' has thus become less about thinking critically and more about blindly accepting a single narrative about how best to handle the pandemic. *This was the first failure of public health for protecting children* – the dismissal of perspectives such as focused protection, which actively considered children's health and wellness.
- Given what we have observed during the response to the COVID-19 crisis, it may be necessary to add a caveat to the three principles. The caveat must call attention to situations where the negligence of adults interferes with the actualization of these three principles in the classroom and results in harm to children.

References

Abaluck, J., Kwong, L.H., Styczynski, A. et al. (2021). *The impact of community masking on COVID-19: A cluster-randomized trial in Bangladesh*. Discussion Papers. 1086. https://elischolar.library.yale.edu/egcenter-discussion-paper-series/1086.

Alwan, N.A., Burgess, R.A., Ashworth, S. et al. (2020, October 31). *The Lancet*, *396*(10260), E71–E72. https://doi.org/10.1016/S0140-6736(20)32153-X

Arim, R., Findlay, L., & Kohen, D. (2020). *The impact of the COVID-19 pandemic on Canadian families of children with disabilities. StatCan COVID-19: Data to Insights for a Better Canada*. https://www150.statcan.gc.ca/n1/pub/45-28-0001/2020001/article/00066-eng.htm

Aurini, J., & Davies, S. (2021). COVID-19 school closures and educational achievement gaps in Canada: Lessons from Ontario summer learning research. *Canadian Review of Sociology/Revue canadienne de sociologie*, *58*, 165–185. https://doi.org/10.1111/cars.12334

Betkowski, B. (2020, November 19). Pandemic putting young readers behind learning curve, says education expert. *University of Alberta FOLIO magazine*. Retrieved December 1 from https://www.ualberta.ca/folio/2020/11/pandemic-putting-young-readers-behind-the-learning-curve-says-education-expert.html

Bhattacharya, J., Gupta, S., & Kulldorff, M. (2020). *Focused Protection*. Retrieved September 15, 2020 from https://gbdeclaration.org/focused-protection/.

Brant, J. (2020, May 1). Racial segregation of Indigenous People in Canada. *The Canadian Encyclopedia*. Retrieved September 12, 2021 from https://www.thecanadianencyclopedia.ca/en/article/racial-segregation-of-indigenous-peoples-in-canada

Bronfenbrenner, U., & Ceci, S.J. (1994). Nature-nuture reconceptualized in developmental perspective: A bioecological model. *Psychological Review*, *101*(4), 568–586. https://doi.org/10.1037/0033-295X.101.4.568

Browne, N.T., Snethen, J.A., Greenberg, C.S., Frenn, M., Kilanowski, J.F., Gance-Cleveland, B., Burke, P.J., & Lewandowski, L. (2021). When pandemics collide: The impact of COVID-19 on childhood obesity. *Journal of Pediatric Nursing*, *56*, 90–98. https://doi.org/10.1016/j.pedn.2020.11.004

Bucerius, S.M., Roberts, B.W., & Jones, D.J. (2021). The effect of the COVID-19 pandemic on domestic violence and child abuse: This article is related directly to the 6th International Law Enforcement & Public Health (LEPH) Virtual Conference in March 2021. *Journal of Community Safety and Well-Being*, *6*(2), 75–79. https://doi.org/10.35502/jcswb.204

Bunis, D., & Rough, J. (2021, September 27). List of coronavirus-related restrictions in every state. Politics and society. AARP. Retrieved September 27 from https://www.aarp.org/politics-society/government-elections/info-2020/coronavirus-state-restrictions.html

Burki, T.K. (2020, November 24). Herd immunity for COVID-19. *The Lancet (Respiratory Medicine). Spotlight, 9*(2), 135–136. https://doi.org/10.1016/S2213-2600(20)30555-5

Children First Canada. (2021, July 30). *Statement regarding Alberta lifting public health restrictions during COVID-10 pandemic.* Retrieved August 15 from https://childrenfirstcanada.org/press-releases/statement-regarding-alberta-lifting-public-health-restrictions-during-covid-19-pandemic/

Cost, K.T., Crosbie, J., Anagnostou, E. et al. (2021). Mostly worse, occasionally better: Impact of COVID-19 pandemic on the mental health of Canadian children and adolescents. *European Child & Adolescent Psychiatry.* https://doi.org/10.1007/s00787-021-01744-3 Retrieved September 1, 2021 from https://link.springer.com/article/10.1007/s00787-021-01744-3#citeas

CTV News Edmonton Staff. (2021, September 28). *Alberta children have the highest rate of active COVID-19 cases of any age group.* Retrieved September 28 from https://edmonton.ctvnews.ca/-alberta-children-have-the-highest-rate-of-active-covid-19-cases-of-any-age-group-1.5603974

Dawson, P., Worrell, M.C., Malone, S. et al. (2020). Pilot investigation of SARS-CoV-2 secondary transmission in kindergarten through Grade 12 schools implementing mitigation strategies – St. Louis County and City of Springfield, Missouri. *Morbidity and Mortality Weekly Report, 70*(12), 449–455. https://doi.org/10.15585/mmwr.mm7012e4

Deoni, S.C.L., Beauchemin, J., Volpe, A., D'Sa, V., & RESONANCE Consortium (2021). Impact of the COVID-19 pandemic on early child cognitive development: Initial findings in a longitudinal observational study of child health. Pre-print submission to Developmental Cognitive Neuroscience. Retrieved September 1, 2021 from https://www.medrxiv.org/content/10.1101/2021.08.10.21261846v1.

Ezpeleta, L., Navarro, J.B., de la Osa, N., Trepat, E., & Penelo, E. (2020). Life conditions during COVID-19 lockdown and mental health in Spanish adolescents. *International Journal of Environmental Research and Public Health, 17*(19), 7327. https://doi.org/10.3390/ijerph17197327

Falk, A., Benda, A., Falk, P. et al. (2021). COVID-19 cases and transmission in 17 K-12 schools – Wood County, Wisconsin, August 31–November 29, 2020. *MMWR Morbidity and Mortality Weekly Report, 70*(4), 136–140. Retrieved from https://dx.doi.org/10.15585/mmwr.mm7004e3

Frenette, M., Frank, K., & Deng, Z. (2020). *COVID-19 Pandemic: School closures and the online preparedness of children. StatCan*

COVID-19: Data to insights for a better Canada. https://www150. statcan.gc.ca/n1/pub/45-28-0001/2020001/article/00001-eng.htm

Gadermann, A.C., Thomson, K.C., Richardson, C.G. et al. (2021). Examining the impacts of the COVID-19 pandemic on family mental health in Canada: Findings from a national cross-sectional study. *BMJ Open*, *11*, e042871. https://doi.org/10.1136/bmjopen-2020–042871

Garcia de Avila, M.A., Hamamoto Filho, P.T., Jacob, F. et al. (2020). Children's anxiety and factors related to the COVID-19 pandemic: An exploratory study using the children's anxiety questionnaire and the numerical rating scale. *International Journal of Environmental Research and Public Health*, *17*(16), 1–13. https://doi.org/10.3390/ijerph17165757.

Government of Canada. (2021). *COVID-19 daily epidemiology update*. Retrieved on September 24, 2021 from https://health-infobase.canada.ca/covid-19/epidemiological-summary-covid-19-cases.html.

Green, J., Staff, L., Bromley, P., Jones, L., & Petty, J. (2021). The implications of face masks for babies and families during the COVID-19 pandemic: A discussion paper. *Journal of Neonatal Nursing: JNN*, *27*(1), 21–25. https://doi.org/10.1016/j.jnn.2020.10.005

Greenlee, E., & Reid, A. (2020). *Parents supporting learning at home during the COVID-19 pandemic. StatCan COVID-19: Data to Insights for a Better Canada.* https://www150.statcan.gc.ca/n1/pub/45-28-0001/2020001/article/00040-eng.htm

Hamwey, M., Allen, L., Hay, M., & Varpio, L. (2019). Bronfenbrenner's bioecological model of human development: Applications for health professions education. *Academic Medicine: Journal of the Association of American Medical Colleges*, *94*(10), 1621. https://doi.org/10.1097/ACM.0000000000002822

Haring, U., Sorin, R., & Caltabiano, N.J. (2019). Reflecting on childhood and child agency in history. *Palgrave Communications*, *5*(52), 1–9. https://doi.org/10.1057/s41599-019-0259-0

Heneghan, C., & Kulldorff, M. (2021, September 15). Stanford faculty smear professor who accurately summarized data on masks. *The Federalist*. Retrieved September 15, 2021 from https://thefederalist.com/2021/09/15/stanford-faculty-smear-professor-who-accurately-summarized-data-on-masks/

Kempe, C.H., Silverman, F.N., Steele, B.F., Droegemueller, W., & Silver, H.K. (1962). The battered-child syndrome. *JAMA*, *181*, 17–24. https://doi.org/10.1001/jama.1962.03050270019004

Kohlberg, E., & Neyman, A. (2020). *Demystifying the math of the coronavirus. Working Paper 20–112.* Harvard Business School.

Harvard University. Retrieved August 15, 2021 from https://www.hbs.edu/ris/Publication%20Files/20-112_4278525d-ccf2-4f8a-b564-2e95d0e7ca5b.pdf

Kulldorff, M., Gupta, S., & Bhattacharya, J. (2020). *The Great Barrington declaration*. Retrieved September 15, 2020 from https://gbdeclaration.org/.

Leighton, J.P. (2020, May 15). Helping your children get through the COVID-19 lockdown. University of Alberta. Speakers' Bureau Online. https://www.ualberta.ca/external-relations/projects-initiatives/speakers-bureau/speakers-bureau-online.html

Leonhardt, D. (2021, June 18). Kids, Covid, and Delta. *New York Times*. The Morning Newsletter. https://www.nytimes.com/2021/06/18/briefing/kids-covid-and-delta.html

Lopatina, O.L., Komleva, Y.K., Gorina, Y.V., Higashida, H., & Salmina, A.B. (2018). Neurobiological aspects of face recognition: The role of oxytocin. *Frontiers in Behavioral Neuroscience*, *12*, Article 195. https://doi.org/10.3389/fnbeh.2018.00195

Macdonald, N.E., Stanwick, R., & Lynk, A. (2014). Canada's shameful history of nutrition research on residential school children: The need for strong medical ethics in Aboriginal health research. *Paediatrics & Child Health*, *19*(2), 64. https://doi.org/10.1093/pch/19.2.64

MacIntyre, C.R., Seale, H., Dung, T.C., Hien, N.T., Nga, P.T., Chughtai, A.A., Rahman, B., Dwyer, D.E., & Wang, Q. (2015). A cluster randomised trial of cloth masks compared with medical masks in healthcare workers. *BMJ Open*, *5*(4), e006577. https://doi.org/10.1136/bmjopen-2014-006577

Mahase, E. (2020). Covid-19: Why are age and obesity risk factors for serious disease? *BMJ 2020*, *371*, 1–2. https://doi.org/10.1136/bmj.m4130

Marshall, T., & Gallant, D. (June 1, 2021). Residential schools in Canada. *The Canadian Encyclopedia*. Retrieved September 12, 2021 from https://www.thecanadianencyclopedia.ca/en/article/residential-schools

Marshall, T., & Robertson, G. (2019, June 7). Eugenics in Canada. *The Canadian Encyclopedia*. Retrieved September 12, 2021 from https://www.thecanadianencyclopedia.ca/en/article/eugenics

Maslow, A.H. (1943). A theory of human motivation. *Psychological Review*, *50*(4), 370–396. https://doi.org/10.1037/h0054346

Mcmaster, G. (2020, May 4). Why COVID-19 loneliness can be especially hard on teens. University of Alberta FOLIO. Retrieved September 1, 2021 from https://www.ualberta.

ca/folio/2020/05/why-covid-19-loneliness-can-be-especially-hard-on-teens.html

Morelli, M., Cattelino, E., Baiocco, R., Trumello, C., Babore, A., Candelori, C., & Chirumbolo, A. (2020). Parents and children during the COVID-19 lockdown: The Influence of parenting distress and parenting self-Efficacy on children's emotional well-being. *Frontiers in Psychology*, *11*, 1–10. https://doi.org/10.3389/fpsyg.2020.584645

Mullen, E. M. (1995). *Mullen scales of early learning* (AGS ed.). Circle Pines, MN: American Guidance Service Inc.

Ontario Agency for Health Protection and Promotion (Public Health Ontario) (2021). Mask wearing in children and COVID-19 – What we know so far. Toronto, ON: Queen's Printer for Ontario. Retrieved September 1, 2021 from https://www.publichealthontario.ca/-/media/documents/ncov/covid-wwksf/2021/08/wwksf-wearing-masks-children.pdf?sc_lang=en

Peetz, C. (2021, September 22). MCPS students' math proficiency, literacy plummet after year of virtual classes. *Bethesda Beat*. Retrieved September 22 from https://bethesdamagazine.com/bethesda-beat/schools/mcps-students-math-proficiency-literacy-plummet-after-year-of-virtual-classes/

Pianta, R.C. (2016). Teacher–student interactions: Measurement, impacts, improvement, and policy. *Policy Insights from the Behavioral and Brain Sciences*, *3*(1), 98–105. https://doi.org/10.1177/2372732215622457

Ravens-Sieberer, U., Kaman, A., Erhart, M., Devine, J., Schlack, R., & Otto, C. (2021). Impact of the COVID-19 pandemic on quality of life and mental health in children and adolescents in Germany. *European Child & Adolescent Psychiatry*, 1–11. Advance online publication. https://doi.org/10.1007/s00787-021-01726-5

Saurabh, K., & Ranjan, S. (2020). Compliance and psychological impact of quarantine in children and adolescents due to Covid-19 pandemic. *Indian Journal of Pediatrics*, *87*(7), 532–536. https://doi.org/10.1007/s12098-020-03347-3

Scott, L., Pascalis, O., & Nelson, C. (2007). A domain general theory of perceptual development. *Current Directions in Psychological Science*, *16*, 197–201. https://doi.org/10.1111/j.1467-8721.2007.00503.x

Sethna, V., Pote, I., Wang, S., et al. (2017). Mother–infant interactions and regional brain volumes in infancy: An MRI study. *Brain Structure and Function*, *222*, 2379–2388. https://doi.org/10.1007/s00429-016-1347-1

Shaw, M., & De Jong, M. (2012). Child abuse and neglect: A major public health issue and the role of child and adolescent mental health services [Editorial]. *The Psychiatrist*, 36(9), 321–325. https://doi.org/10.1192/pb.bp.111.037135

Simion, F., & Giorgio, E.D. (2015). Face perception and processing in early infancy: Inborn predispositions and developmental changes. *Frontiers in Psychology*, 2015.6. https://doi.org/10.3389/fpsyg.2015.00969.

Spinelli, M., Lionetti, F., Pastore, M., & Fasolo, M. (2020). Parents' stress and children's psychological problems in families facing the COVID-19 outbreak in Italy. *Frontiers in Psychology*, 11, 1713. https://doi.org/10.3389/fpsyg.2020.01713

Spitzer, M. (2020). Masked education? The benefits and burdens of wearing face masks in schools during the current Corona pandemic. *Trends in Neuroscience and Education*, 20, 100138. https://doi.org/10.1016/j.tine.2020.100138.

Staples, K., MacDonald, M., & Zimmer, C. (2012). Chapter Seven – Assessment of motor behavior among children and adolescents with autism spectrum disorder. International *Review of Research in Developmental Disabilities*, 42, 179–214.

Statistics Canada. (2021). *Canadian Community Health Survey, 2019, Canadian Perspectives Survey Series 1, Canadian Perspectives Survey Series 4*. Retrieved August 15, 2021 from https://www150.statcan.gc.ca/n1/pub/11-631-x/2020004/s3-eng.htm.

Stern, A.M. (2005). Sterilized in the name of public health: Race, immigration, and reproductive control in modern California. *American Journal of Public Health*, 95(7), 1128–1138. https://doi.org/10.2105/AJPH.2004.041608

Tervalon, M., & Murray-García, J. (1998). Cultural humility versus cultural competence: A critical distinction in defining physician training outcomes in multicultural education. *Journal of Health Care for the Poor and Underserved*, 9(2), 117–125. https://doi.org/10.1353/hpu.2010.0233

Thomas, E.Y., Anurudran, A., Robb, K., & Burke, T.F. (2020). Spotlight on child abuse and neglect response in the time of COVID-19. *The Lancet. Public Health*, 5(7), 1–2 e371. https://doi.org/10.1016/S2468-2667(20)30143-2

Tierney, A.L., & Nelson, C.A. (2009). Brain development and the role of experience in the early years. *Zero to Three*, 30(2), 9–13. Retrieved September 30, 2021 from https://www.ncbi.nlm.nih.gov/pmc/articles/PMC3722610/

UN General Assembly (November 20, 1989). Convention on the Rights of the Child, United Nations, *Treaty Series*, vol. 1577, p. 3. Retrieved May 25, 2021 from www.refworld.org/docid/3ae6b38f0. html.

United Nations. (2020). *Policy brief: Covid-19 and the need for action on mental health.* New York: United Nations.

Vlachos, J., Hertegård, E., & Svaleryd, H.B. (2021). The effects of school closures on SARS-CoV-2 among parents and teachers. *Proceedings of the National Academy of Sciences of the United States of America*, 118(9), e2020834118. https://doi.org/10.1073/pnas. 2020834118

Waddell, B. (2021, September 14). A look at school mask mandates by state. U.S. News and World Report. Retrieved September 20, 2021 from https://www.usnews.com/news/best-states/articles/2021-09-14/school-mask-mandates-by-state.

Waechter, R., Kumanayaka, D., Angus-Yamada, C., Wekerle, C., Smith, S., & MAP Research Team (2019). Maltreatment history, trauma symptoms and research reactivity among adolescents in child protection services. *Child and Adolescent Psychiatry and Mental Health*, 13, 1–10. https://doi.org/10.1186/s13034-019-0270-7

Willyard, C. (2021). COVID and schools: The evidence for reopening safely. *Nature*, 595(7866), 164–167. https://doi.org/10.1038/ d41586-021-01826-x

Winston, R., & Chicot, R. (2016). The importance of early bonding on the long-term mental health and resilience of children. *London Journal of Primary Care*, 8(1), 12–14. https://doi.org/10.1080/ 17571472.2015.1133012

World Health Organization. (2020). Advice on the use of masks for children in the community in the context of COVID-19: Annex to the advice on the use of masks in the context of context of COVID-19. Geneva: World Health Organization. Retrieved September 24, 2021 from https://www.who.int/publications/i/item/WHO-2019-nCoV-IPC_Masks-Children-2020

Yogman, M., Garner, A., Hutchinson, J., Hirsh-Pasek, K., Golinkoff, R.M., Committee on Psychosocial Aspects of Child and Family Health, & Council on Communications and Media. (2018). The power of play: A pediatric role in enhancing development in young children. *Pediatrics*, 142(3), 1–17.

Zhou, S.J., Zhang, L.G., Wang, L.L. et al. (2020). Prevalence and socio-demographic correlates of psychological health problems in Chinese adolescents during the outbreak of COVID-19. *European of Child & Adolescent Psychiatry, 29,* 749–758. https://doi. org/10.1007/s00787-020-01541-4

Zimmerman, K.O., Akinboyo, I.C., Brookhart, M.A., Boutzoukas, A.E., McGann, K.A., Smith, M.J., Maradiaga Panayotti, G., Armstrong, S.C., Bristow, H., Parker, D., Zadrozny, S., Weber, D.J., Benjamin, D.K., Jr, & ABC Science Collaborative (2021). Incidence and secondary transmission of SARS-CoV-2 infections in schools. *Pediatrics, 147*(4), e2020048090. https://doi.org/10.1542/ peds.2020-048090

Zweig, D. (2021, August 20). The science of masking kids at school remains uncertain. *New York Magazine's Intelligencer.* Retrieved September 1, 2021 from https://nymag.com/intelligencer/2021/08/- the-science-of-masking-kids-at-school-remains-uncertain.html

Index

Note: **Bold** page numbers refer to tables; *italic* page numbers refer to figures and page numbers followed by "n" denote endnotes.